KiDS 'N VALUES

A HANDBOOK FOR HELPING KIDS DISCOVER CHRISTIAN VALUES

JOHN A. FLANAGAN

LIGUORI
PUBLICATIONS

One Liguori Drive
Liguori, Missouri 63057-9999
(314) 464-2500

ISBN 0-89243-411-2
Library of Congress Catalog Card Number: 91-62268

Copyright © 1992, Liguori Publications
Printed in U.S.A.

Cover and interior art by Chris Sharp

Contents

Discover values every day,
In each experience on your way.
Whether old or whether new,
Every value is part of you.

Introduction

■ VALUES are basic components of our daily lives. Some of our values are highly personal and uniquely ours. Some of our values align with the values of others and are easily recognized in words and behaviors.

Values constitute a major dimension of who we are. We understand ourselves better and choose appropriate ways of living when we have a firm grasp on our values. They influence and form our lives.

Values are first discovered in infancy. The infant receives or accepts the breast or bottle — and responds by sucking and receiving food and nourishment. This cycle of receiving and responding can be called an "experience." The baby makes an automatic valuing response to the experience: "Yum, this is good." From that point on, food and nourishment are a value to that human being.

As other experiences come into the child's life, the valuing process becomes more complex. By the time the child enters school, value decisions are based on the immediate experience plus the residue of many past experiences and the values that grew out of them.

When values are first experienced, they must be evaluated: "Do I want to make this or that value a part of my overall character? Is this something I want to live by? Do I want this value to influence my decisions?" Before values can be appraised, however, they must be discovered.

Discovering values is a lifelong endeavor. From simple beginnings, the number and complexity of values explode by nine or ten years of age. The child explores beyond the confines of home and finds a constantly expanding environment. Parents, youth ministers, religious educators, and teachers do well to help young people discover values — as many as they can — from age seven through age twelve. As adults, it's our responsibility to help youngsters recognize values and sort through them according to their overall positive and negative effects. For many of us, this may be a difficult endeavor, especially if we've never engaged in any process of value assessment.

We begin with an understanding of two kinds of values. Try to appreciate these two kinds of values as a nine- or ten-year-old youngster would.

Inside values: These are inner dispositions regarding the way a person wants to see himself or herself. They begin with an orientation within the individual and are manifested in choices made.

Imagine a child struggling with the following:

Inside value: I want to be cool. I may get caught stealing that jacket, but it's worth it.
Outside value: If I wear trendy clothes, I show others that I'm cool.

See how convoluted one's understanding of values can become?

- I want to be a good student. I may have to work hard, but it's worth it.
- I want to be responsible when I'm left on my own. I may not be able to do exactly what I want to do, but it's worth it.
- I want to be kind. I may have to be courteous when I don't want to be, but it's worth it.
- I want to be dependable. I may have to give up goofing off and being lazy, but it's worth it.

These are strong, positive, and powerfully influential values. Recognizing their strengths and choosing them day by day give the child a solid value system to rely on well into the teen and adult years.

Outside values: These are outer actions performed for the purpose of making a personal statement about one's character. They make a statement about the way an individual wants to be in society.

- If I share one little thing with someone who needs it, I show others that I am an unselfish person.
- If I refuse to cheat, I show others that I am an honest person.
- If I help others with their chores, I show others that I am a loving person.
- If I do what my parents and teachers expect, I show others that I am maturing.

One major factor influencing our perceptions of values and our ability to determine their respective negative and positive weight is our attitude. Attitudes are learned predispositions toward persons, things, events, or circumstances. We are not born with these predispositions; rather, they are formed within us by our interaction with our cultural milieu and immediate surroundings.

The forming elements of these predispositions are experiences generated by stimuli. A stimulus — a thing, person, or event — is presented; we receive the stimulus and respond. That stimulus is repeated or other stimuli are presented, and again we receive and respond: receiving/responding; receiving/responding; receiving/responding. While these receiving/responding patterns are forming the experiences of our lives, we engage in a valuing process of assessing each experience: "I want that experience again; I'd rather not have that experience again."

Each experience comes to us through two basic channels: the visual channel (reading, media, nature, the behavior of others) and the audio channel (media, nature, and verbal exchanges with others). Teachers, religious educators, youth leaders, and parents help youngsters discover and form positive values by engaging them in dialogues and discussions following visual or audio experiences. These moments are ripe with values waiting to be discovered and assessed — if the adult will merely seize the opportunity with and for the youngster.

Our objective — and responsibility — is to help kids understand what their own attitudes are, how their experiences have formed their attitudes and influenced their value system, and how the subsequent choices they make affect their lives and the world around them. By way of repetition, discussion, singing, role-playing, storytelling, and just plain fun, you can alert youngsters to the myriad of values that exists in our culture. You can introduce them to the reality of conflicting value systems. You can teach them to recognize what's at risk when value systems collide. Finally, you can help youngsters get in touch with their own wisdom and strength to know and choose behavior consistent with a positive and faith-filled value system.

The exercises that follow use both the visual and audio channels of experiencing. To assist you in using this material, Liguori Publications invites you to take advantage of the blanket photocopy permission offered in the front of this book. You may photocopy any of the following pages for use in your family, classroom, retreat setting, or youth group. Before you use any of the exercises, review with the kids the distinction between inside and outside values. Also, remind the youngsters that in the process of discussing and discovering values, there are no right or wrong answers. Everyone has something to contribute. As the adult facilitator, you must be especially sensitive to this fact.

You may give them your love but not your thoughts,
For they have their own thoughts.
You may house their bodies but not their souls,
For their souls dwell in the house of tomorrow,
Which you cannot visit, not even in your dreams.
You may strive to be like them,
But seek not to make them like you,
For life goes not backward nor tarries with yesterday.
You are the bows from which your children as living arrows
Are sent forth.
Kahlil Gibran

Tell me a story
About what people do
When they act out their values
Just like me and you.

Vignettes

■ VIGNETTES are brief stories. As we focus on the action and characters in these stories, we will discover values.

After you've read a vignette to/with the young people, discuss with them the obvious and the not-so-obvious values being portrayed. Once the values are identified, begin an evaluation process which gives the youngsters an opportunity to reflect on those values that are especially positive. This greater awareness increases their ability to organize values and see how values work in their lives.

Each vignette concludes with a set of questions. Use these questions to stimulate discussion — but remain flexible. These are not the only questions that might spark discussion. Spontaneous questions, comments, and insights will be generated out of the discussion itself. Explore each person's contribution with respect. Remember: values are being discovered.

Stories have been used from ancient times to the present to teach children — and adults — to identify elements of right and wrong in human behavior. Vignettes lead quickly to such identification.

■ TOMMY walked quickly down the hall toward his fifth-grade classroom. He was excited because yesterday he'd been named student of the month for the whole school. To win that honor, Tommy had to have good grades and outstanding behavior. Tommy had worked hard on his studies and was very careful to be courteous and responsible. His mom and dad were so proud of him that the family was going out to celebrate.

As he walked down the hall, he glanced up to find the principal, Mr. Evans, smiling at him.

"Good morning, Tommy," he said.

"Good morning, Mr. Evans," Tommy returned the greeting with a cheery smile.

Passing Mr. Evans brought Tommy to the corner where he turned down the hall to his classroom. The hall was empty, but there it was on the floor. Tommy stooped to pick it up.

"Wow! A twenty-dollar bill!" he whispered to himself with disbelief. "I could buy a horn for my bike. Or I could order two hot-fudge sundaes together — and no one could tell me I couldn't! Or how about those neat mixing bowls Mom's been wanting. I could surprise her with them."

Tommy looked at the bill for a moment longer, then folded it and stuck it into the pocket of his jeans. He looked up and down the hall. The hall was still empty; no one had seen him. Twenty dollars was more money than he had ever had at one time in his whole life. What should he do with it?

What is one value inside of Tommy? How do you know?

What is one value outside of Tommy? How do you know?

What is one value inside of Tommy that will help him make a right choice about the money?

What is one value outside of Tommy that will show others that he has good values?

Make a list of all the values you think Tommy has.

_____   _____

_____   _____

_____   _____

What values of your own could help you decide what to do with the twenty-dollar bill if you were the one to find it?

_____   _____

_____   _____

_____   _____

■PEGGY is the best student in the fourth grade. She has earned all A's on every report card and now the year is almost over. Today is the last math test, and Peggy wants so badly to do well.

"I wish I were as smart as you," Alice tells her in the hall.

"Yeah, what a brain!" adds Nancy.

"Yeah, brain is right!" chimes in Joe as he walks by.

The kids' remarks really delight Peggy. They make her want to do even better. But Peggy is uneasy about this test. She has not studied for it. Her grandmother who lives with her and her family — and is Peggy's favorite person in all the world — has become very ill. The whole family is worried, and Peggy has cried herself to sleep the past two nights. She feels very tired.

That morning at breakfast, Peggy's dad had given her a warm hug. "Hey, chin up, Peggy girl," he'd said. "Grandma had a good night. Now you need to have a good day!"

When the teacher hands out the test, Peggy sees her worst fear come to life. There are only three problems, and she has forgotten how to do one of them. She works two problems quickly but can't even get started on the third. Bob, a super math student, sits across from her. She can see his paper, and he's working on number three without any struggle. It would be easy to cheat. How right or wrong would that be?

What is one value inside of Peggy? How do you know?

What is one value outside of Peggy? How do you know?

What is one value inside of Peggy that will help her make a right choice about cheating on the math test?

What is one value outside of Peggy that will show others that she has good values?

Make a list of all the values you think Peggy has.

_____   _____

_____   _____

_____   _____

What values of your own could help you decide what to do with the problem of cheating on the math test?

_____   _____

_____   _____

_____   _____

■CARL was the bully of the playground. He had pushed or punched or pinched or shoved or scratched or harassed almost every youngster on the playground. If someone told a teacher, Carl would catch that person away from school to get even. One day Carl noticed Pablo. He walked up to him and slapped him on the shoulder.

"Hi, Pablo. They say you're tough."

"Not me, man," Pablo replied. "I'm just a nice guy."

"Oh, yeah? Well, I want to know how tough a nice guy can be. I want you to decide when you're going to fight me," ordered Carl.

"I don't want to fight you," replied Pablo.

"I know you don't, but you're gonna," Carl warned.

Pablo walked away, but he knew Carl would continue to bother him. He also knew he was stronger and quicker than Carl. His older brothers had taught him how to fight.

Two days later, Carl came up to Pablo after school and punched him on the arm. A few seconds later, Carl punched him again. Pablo finally turned to face the grinning bully.

"You decided when we're gonna fight?" Carl sneered.

"Not yet," answered Pablo as he moved quickly down the sidewalk. Carl did not follow him.

Pablo thought to himself, "Maybe if I fight him, he'll leave me alone."

Is this the right thing to do?

What is one value inside of Pablo? How do you know?

What is one value outside of Carl? How do you know?

What is one value inside of Pablo that will help him make a right choice about fighting Carl?

What is one value outside of Pablo that will show others that he has good values?

Make a list of all the values you think Pablo has. Make a list of all the values you think Carl has.

PABLO	**CARL**
_____	_____
_____	_____
_____	_____

What values of your own could help you decide what to do about fighting Carl if you were in Pablo's place?

_____	_____
_____	_____
_____	_____

■ MANDY and René were late getting to school. When they cut across a lawn on their way to school, a lady rushed out of the house and began scolding them. "You girls stay off my lawn," she warned. "There are sidewalks — use them!"

Without saying a word, the girls hurried on their way.

"That old witch is always yelling at me when I take a shortcut," René grumbled angrily.

"Well, we did walk on her grass," Mandy reminded René.

"Yeah, but we didn't hurt it," René argued.

The girls walked on without saying anything more. As they neared the school, René spoke again. "Hey, I'd like to teach that ol' witch a lesson. My dad has some stuff that kills grass. Let's go by tonight and spill some on her grass!"

Mandy laughed with René about her suggestion. Then she began to realize that René was serious; René really did want to ruin the lady's lawn.

"You don't really want to do that, do you?" Mandy asked.

"I sure do!" declared René.

"Don't be silly, René. Why ruin her lawn?"

"Just to tell that old lady to quit screaming at me," René insisted.

What should Mandy do?

What is one value inside of René? How do you know?

What is one value outside of René? How do you know?

What is one value inside of Mandy that will help her make a right choice about ruining the lady's lawn?

What is one value outside of Mandy that will show others that she has good values?

Make a list of all the values you think René has. Make a list of all the values you think Mandy has.

RENÉ	MANDY
_____	_____
_____	_____
_____	_____

What values of your own could help you decide what to do about ruining the lady's lawn?

_____   _____

_____   _____

_____   _____

■ JASON moved into town just in time to try out for one of the soccer teams. He played well and was accepted instantly by team members and coaches. Jason's father had played soccer all his life and had taught his son well.

The day of the first game was exciting for Jason. His team won — and he scored the only two goals. He couldn't wait to tell his dad, who was away on a business trip.

That afternoon was the first time Jason had walked home with any of the other boys. Bob, Larry, and Jack invited him to walk with them, and he was glad to accept. As they passed the convenience store, Bob elbowed Jason. "Hey, Jason, I dare you to snatch a candy bar."

"Not me," Jason answered quickly.

"Come on, Jason, we do it all the time," Larry baited him.

"Yeah, Jase, we're the four best players. We have to do things together," added Jack.

"We don't have to steal, though," Jason declared.

"Oh, they got lots of candy bars," urges Jack. "They won't miss one once in a while."

"I don't have to steal," Jason repeated.

Jason felt certain that if he didn't go along, he'd have trouble keeping the boys as his friends. How important is belonging to this group?

What is one value inside of Jason? How do you know?

What is one value outside of Jason? How do you know?

What is one value inside of Jason that will help him make a right choice about his friendships?

What is one value outside of Jason that will show others that he has good values?

Make a list of all the values you think Jason has.

_____   _____

_____   _____

_____   _____

What values of your own could help you decide what to do about a friendship with these three boys?

_____   _____

_____   _____

_____   _____

■MARIA'S great-aunt was very old and moved into a nursing home a month ago. Maria is ten years old and remembers the many happy days she spent with her great-aunt before she had to be moved to the nursing home. She and her Great-aunt Martha had been very close to each other.

"You must be pretty busy these days," remarked Aunt Martha. "You haven't been to see me for ten days."

Maria didn't feel she could tell her great-aunt the real reason for not visiting, so she agreed. "Yeah, I've been pretty busy," Maria mumbled. "I'll try to get here more, though." She felt guilty.

Maria didn't like to come to the nursing home because of two old ladies she had to pass to get to her great-aunt's room. Each time she came to the nursing home, these ladies tried to stop her and touch her.

"Oh, you're so beautiful. Can't I give you a big hug?" one of them would ask.

"Why don't you give old Rachel a little kiss," the other would say.

Maria wanted to see her great-aunt, but she hated the attention of these ladies. She went to the nurse's station.

"Is there another way to get in here to see my great-aunt," she asked, "besides walking down this hall?"

"No, this is the only way," the nurse answered with a smile.

Maria skipped down the hall, passed the two ladies as they called to her, and quickly bounced out the exit.

What's the right thing to do?

What is one value inside of Maria? How do you know?

What is one value outside of Maria? How do you know?

What is one value inside of Maria that will help her make a right choice about visiting her great-aunt?

What is one value outside of Maria that will show others that she has good values?

Make a list of all the values you think Maria has.

_____   _____

_____   _____

_____   _____

What values of your own could help you decide what to do about visiting your aunt if you were in Maria's place?

_____   _____

_____   _____

_____   _____

■MRS. KINTZ had divided her fifth grade into groups of five to work together on a special project. Eric ended up with three of the smarter girls and Ben. Ben was from Mexico. His parents had recently been given permits to seek naturalization as citizens. They lived in the old trailer court.

The three girls began calling him "Black Ben" behind his back. They complained about being put in a group with Ben.

"His skin is so dark and dirty looking," complained Cathy.

"Yeah, and he talks funny. That is when he talks at all," added Louise.

"But he's in our group," Eric reminded them.

"That's the problem," stormed Judy. "He's in our group and we don't want to work with him. I won't work with him. I don't want to be anywhere near him."

The other two girls agreed.

"Hey, you're nuts!" declared Eric. "Ben's a good kid, and if you don't help, we'll do the project by ourselves."

"That's okay," said Judy. "Mrs. Kintz will still give us credit."

"Not if she knows you didn't do any work," Eric warned.

"You mean you'd tell? That's the only way she would find out, isn't it?" asked Louise.

"If you don't help, I might tell," Eric answered.

What's right or wrong about Eric's reaction?

What is one value inside of Eric? How do you know?

What is one value outside of Eric? How do you know?

What is one value inside of Eric that will help him make a right choice about what to do in his group?

What is one value outside of Eric that will show others that he has good values?

Make a list of all the values you think Eric has.

_____   _____

_____   _____

_____   _____

What values of your own could help you decide what to do if you were in Eric's place?

_____   _____

_____   _____

_____   _____

■HIS MOTHER called him Luigi. His friends shortened it to Lu. His dog trailed at his heels wherever he went. He called his dog Hobo because he just came by one day and never left.

One day, when Luigi and Hobo were walking down the sidewalk, two boys threw rocks at Hobo. Luigi ran to them.

"Don't you never throw rocks at Hobo!" Luigi shouted. "You hear me? Never!"

Luigi was small but very strong. The boys looked at him and began laughing. One tossed another rock at Hobo, who growled.

"No, Hobo," said Luigi. "You sit."

Hobo sat and Luigi grabbed the boy by his belt and threw him against a fence. The second boy grabbed at Luigi, but he ended up against the fence, too.

"Now, Hobo, do you want your turn?" Luigi asked.

"Just skip it," one boy said. "We're leaving."

"Don't move," Luigi told them. "Stand still. Come, Hobo!"

Both boys backed hard against the fence as Luigi slowly led Hobo toward them.

"Shake," Luigi told Hobo, who faced one boy and raised a paw. The boy carefully took the dog's paw; the other boy did the same.

"Now you know Hobo," Luigi explained. "Don't you never throw rocks or anything at him again!"

Did Luigi do the right thing?

What is one value inside of Luigi? How do you know?

What is one value outside of Luigi? How do you know?

What is one value inside of Luigi that helped him make a right choice about defending Hobo?

What is one value outside of Luigi that will show others that he has good values?

Make a list of all the values you think Luigi has.

_____   _____

_____   _____

_____   _____

What values of your own could help you decide what to do if someone threw rocks at your dog?

_____   _____

_____   _____

_____   _____

■ AMY lived on a farm. Every day she walked down the lane to the road where the school bus picked her up. This morning, as always, she climbs aboard in her jeans and plaid shirt.

"Hey, Amy, do you have any dresses?" Bill asks.

"I don't think it's any of your business," Amy replies.

"Yeah, Bill, it's none of your business if Hayseed Amy wants to look like a tramp," one girl calls from the back of the bus.

"Okay, Barb, your big mouth's open again," Bill answers.

That brings out a lot of remarks from other riders, many of them directed at Amy, who sits in a seat by herself. She quietly bows her head and tries to ignore all that's going on. When the bus stops to pick up other students, the driver turns around and faces the kids. "That's enough of the smart-alec stuff," he orders. "You kids can talk without all the teasing."

As the bus begins moving again, Bill crosses to where Amy is sitting. "Scoot over," he tells Amy. Without a word she slides across the seat to the window. Bill sits down.

"Hey, I'm sorry," he says. "I didn't try to start what happened. I really do want to know if you have any dresses."

Amy blinks her eyes and smiles a little. "Well, I do wear dresses to church on Sunday," she admits.

"Which church?"

"The big one up on the hill," Amy replies.

"Is it okay if I come there Sunday and see you in a dress?"

Did Bill do the right thing?

What is one value inside of Bill? How do you know?

What is one value outside of Amy? How do you know?

What is one value inside of Bill that will help him make right choices about the way he treats other people?

What is one value outside of Bill that will show others he has good values?

Make a list of all the values you think Bill has. Make a list of all the values you think Amy has.

BILL	AMY
_____	_____
_____	_____
_____	_____

What values of your own could help you decide what to do in relating to Amy, who dresses different, or Barb, who is mean?

_____   _____

_____   _____

_____   _____

"Monkey see, monkey do,"
The ancient saying goes.
We see healthy imitation
Of good models that one knows.

Biographies

■A BIOGRAPHY is the account of someone's life. Even brief biographies can be powerfully inspiring and encouraging. Biographies offer positive life models to kids of all ages.

Biographies can be used to help youngsters discover values. To be especially effective, the biographies should include incidents from the childhood and teenage years of the individuals being highlighted. The content may mention events of adult life, but it's important to provide material that the kids can relate to — and youth is one common ground.

Biographies give youngsters excellent models. When we help children look at an Abraham Lincoln or a Joan of Arc or a Bill Cosby, we open for them the front door to maturity. We show them a life model worth imitating. We give them the chance to consider how these great persons handled everyday problems. We give them the chance to seriously consider values that shaped the lives of these individuals.

A discussion guide accompanies each of the following biographies. Once the youngsters are familiar with the biography and understand any confusing or unfamiliar words, be prepared to facilitate a discussion regarding the individual's values and choices. You may want each child to have a page of questions, or a page for each small group may suffice. Encourage the young people to question and read more about each of these individuals. Ask if anyone knows further information about the individual that the biography does not mention. Encourage them to share that information.

When we look at the lives of the following individuals, we see displayed the inside values that their behavior reflected. We need to help children discover the continuity between the inside value and the outside value.

From the hour of birth, the human being's development is fostered by imitation in learning language and mobility. Children seem to extend an unspoken invitation: "Show me so I can do it, too."

■ THE QUARTERBACK had just called a play on the concrete streets of Philadelphia. Bill Cosby went out for the pass. When Bill was nine, his mother worked twelve hours a day to support their family. In an effort to be the man of the house and help his mother, Bill worked shining shoes, stocking shelves, and dusting and cleaning in stores.

In school, Bill enjoyed entertaining his classmates. "I found out how much fun it was to make people laugh. I liked that. I made friends that way." Only one teacher, however, appreciated his humor. The others criticized him.

In high school, creating fun and participating in sports claimed most of his attention. Of course, this brought many failures.

Finally, Bill dropped out of school and joined the navy. When he got out of the navy, something was added to his ability to tell funny stories: he had become a star athlete. He returned to school and earned good grades at Temple University. When a summer job gave him an opportunity to be a stand-up comedian, Bill Cosby left the university to be a comic. He later returned to study hard and earn many degrees.

Cosby became a great comedy star who played television roles, recorded comedy albums, made movies, and produced cartoons and comic strips. The most important thing to Bill Cosby is being a father to his family. As a poor kid from the streets of Philadelphia, he has gone far. He makes an interesting declaration: "I'm interested in just one thing: poor white kids and poor black kids."

Bill Cosby likes to make people laugh. Is that a value? Tell why or why not.

Cosby wants to be a good father to his family. Does this have something to do with his values? Tell how.

Would you want to be like Bill Cosby? Why? In what ways? Why not?

What qualities do you admire in Cosby? Why?

What is there about Bill Cosby that makes him a person you would like to have as a close friend?

Make a list of all the good values you think are part of Bill Cosby's value system.

_____   _____

_____   _____

_____   _____

■ "GIRLS can do anything boys can do, so don't tell me I can't do something because I'm a girl!"

As a ten-year-old, Amelia Earhart was determined to be exactly what she wanted to be. On one occasion she calmed a snarling dog that was even bigger than she. "Lie down," she said. "No one is going to hurt you."

Another time Amelia directed the building of a roller coaster from the top of a barn loft to the ground — which was a considerable distance. When the other three girls who had helped build the roller coaster declined to try it out, Amelia rode down the track on the little car they had built on roller skates.

Amelia also developed her own museum that contained red spiders in a bottle, a big toad in a box, a live garter snake, and other exhibits. Such ventures, along with playing with boys' toys, puzzled her grandmother. But Amelia tried to explain. "Grandma, girls want to play and have fun. They want to be free. They aren't happy just acting like grown-up ladies. There are things to be done and girls want to do them!"

She wrote throughout her life. During World War I, she served as a volunteer nurse in an army hospital. She attended college where she enjoyed a motor mechanics course. She was intrigued with airplanes and became one of the first women pilots. She was the first woman to fly solo across the Atlantic Ocean.

In 1937 she and her copilot were lost while flying over the Pacific Ocean. They were never found.

Were the values of Amelia Earhart the same as the values of older people around her? Tell how they were the same or different.

Would Amelia have been a different kind of person if she had acted just as her grandmother would have liked? Tell how.

What in Amelia's life is similar to something in your life?

What is there about Amelia that makes her a person whom you would like as a close friend?

Make a list of all the good values you think are part of Amelia Earhart.

_____   _____

_____   _____

_____   _____

■ WALT'S FATHER, Elias Disney, ruled his home through fear. Walt's mother and all five of the children knew this fear. Because Elias felt toys were a waste, none were allowed in the Disney house. Without toys, Walt developed a special love for animals that caused him to study their every move.

From age five to nine, Walt lived on the family farm, where he worked every day. This gave him his first chance to know animals. Then his father moved the Disneys to Kansas City, where Elias took on the delivery of three thousand daily newspapers. Walt earned money at various odd jobs and from carrying papers, sometimes through several feet of snow. His father kept all his earnings. "I feed and clothe you. That's enough," he would say. "You're not old enough to handle money, Walter."

Walt was fifteen when Elias sold the paper route. He took all his own money and Walt's savings to buy a jelly factory in Chicago. Walt stayed in Kansas City, however, to finish the school year.

During World War I, sixteen-year-old Walt joined the Red Cross Ambulance Corps. When he returned from the war at eighteen, he left home to begin his career as an artist.

After many lean years, he introduced Mickey Mouse to the world — then Donald Duck, some other characters, and evenutally Snow White. Later, he built Disneyland.

"Disneyland is planned to please everybody," Walt once commented. "People who work there must be happy and polite. It must always be clean."

Was cleanliness a value for Walt Disney? How do you know?

Was studying animals' movements one of Disney's values? How did his interest in animals touch his life?

What right-and-wrong kinds of problems did Disney have to deal with as a youngster?

If we lack something in life, do we sometimes develop a positive value as a result? Did Disney do this? Explain. (Think about him having no toys.)

Could you use any of Walt Disney's values in your life? Tell which values and how you would use them.

Make a list of all the good values you think were part of Walt Disney.

_____   _____

_____   _____

_____   _____

■ SACAGAWEA, a Native American princess, was born in Idaho in 1788. As a member of the Shoshone Indian tribe, she learned all the skills required of a woman. She learned which berries and roots were edible, how to prepare a deerskin and make a dress out of it, how to cut strips of buffalo meat for drying, and how to take down a tepee and erect it in the next camp.

In 1799 the Shoshone tribe was camped near a buffalo herd so they could eat and store dried meat. A Hidatsa war party raided Sacagawea's camp. The young girl was captured and carried away to the Hidatsa village in North Dakota where she was made the slave of a tribal chief. When she was sixteen, the chief lost her in a gamble with a French trader, Touissaint Charbonneau. He made her his wife and she became known as "Charbonneau's woman."

A year later, at seventeen, she was mother of Pompy, a two-month-old baby boy. The Lewis and Clark Expedition, formed to explore the Louisiana Purchase, arrived in her camp. The men had rowed up the Missouri River from St. Louis. An interpreter was going to be needed to bargain for horses when they reached the headwaters of the river. Because that was in Shoshone territory, Sacagawea agreed to go along as interpreter and guide.

The journey was very difficult. Sacagawea never complained, however, and the soldiers in the expedition grew to admire her. She was always excited about new sights and meeting new people. She negotiated for the horses the explorers needed, walked or rode with the men — with Pompy on her back — and shared chores. She volunteered to continue on after reaching her Shoshone tribe. She knew the expedition needed her — and she wanted to see the headwaters of the rivers and the splendid beauty of the Pacific Ocean. She was eager to meet other white folks and to visit other Indian tribes.

She left North Dakota on April 7, 1805, and returned on August 17, 1806. She is still honored for her service to the United States.

What are some of Sacagawea's values? How are some of her values similar to your values today?

Sacagawea accepted her captivity and went about her duties as a slave without complaining. What values of hers do you think this shows?

Would you want to be like Sacagawea? Why or why not?

Sacagawea learned many things that are not often learned today. How was what she learned related to her values?

Make a list of all the good values you think were part of Sacagawea.

_____   _____

_____   _____

_____   _____

■ ABRAHAM LINCOLN was born in Kentucky on a farm. His father, Thomas, moved the family to another Kentucky farm when Abraham was two. They lived there until Abraham was seven. By then, being large for his age and strong, he did a share of the work.

Thomas surprised his family with an announcement one day.

"We're moving to Indiana," he said. "The state will give us a quarter section of land as our own farm."

So they moved. The one-hundred-sixty acres were covered with forest. They arrived late in fall and had to settle for an open shelter with a fire burning constantly to keep them warm through the winter. Abraham began swinging an ax every day to provide firewood. In the spring he was stronger and helped his father split and shape logs for the cabin they built together. This made them happier and more comfortable. Thomas and Abraham worked hard clearing timber for their farm.

About a year later, Abraham's mother, Nancy, became ill and died. They buried her among the trees near the cabin. Abraham was distressed because there was no memorial service. "We really should have had something." Finally, when a traveling preacher prayed at the grave, Lincoln felt better.

For more than a year, the cabin seemed empty and sad. Then his father married again and there were three new children to join Abe and his sister, Sarah.

While in Indiana, Abraham grew from childhood into adulthood. As a teenager, he was six foot four inches tall, lean, and strong. He worked every minute, either for his father or for neighbors.

Abraham studied law, entered politics, and eventually became the sixteenth president of the United States. He was assassinated as he began his second term.

What were some of Abraham Lincoln's values? Are any of them important today? Why are they important?

How did Abraham show his values?

How can we decide if hard work is a value to someone? Is hard work important in the lives of many successful people? What does this say to us?

Do you show any values that Abraham Lincoln showed? Which ones? How do you show them?

What is there about Lincoln that makes him a person you might like to imitate?

Make a list of the good values you think were part of Abraham Lincoln.

_____   _____

_____   _____

_____   _____

■ "I LIKE to hurdle over hedges and race with streetcars," Mildred Didrikson told her older sister, Lillie, as they took turns swinging on a trapeze that hung from a tree in their backyard.

"Oh, I know that," said Lillie. "Just like you want to win all the marbles in town and beat everyone in swimming."

"Yeah! And I want to throw a ball farther and run faster and shoot more baskets and kick a football farther than anyone else, even the boys …especially the boys! I want to win and win!"

That was exactly what Mildred did. She was active, constantly developing her skills — one after the other. Her outstanding ability at baseball caused the boys to choose Mildred first. They also gave her a nickname — Babe, for Babe Ruth, the greatest athletic hero for the children of her day.

When she reached high school, Babe played on every girls' team and did very well. Her sports included volleyball, basketball, baseball, tennis, and swimming. With Babe playing, her high-school basketball team never lost a game. Later, starring for an Amateur Athletic Union women's team, she scored 210 points in five games.

Babe Didrikson was nineteen when she saw her first track meet. She began practicing immediately to be good, not in any one event, but in all of them. She was entered in one Amateur Athletic Union track meet as a one-woman team. Babe won six first places and one fourth place — and the entire meet! Following that, she went to the 1932 Olympics, where she won three medals: two golds and a silver.

Because she wanted to help her parents and her family, Babe put together a traveling show in which she demonstrated athletic skills and played the harmonica. She had practiced on the harmonica since early childhood.

Next, she learned to play golf. She became a professional competitor and a millionaire as a golfer. Even after developing cancer, Babe Didrikson Zaharias continued to play. After her death, many called her the greatest athlete of the twentieth century.

Is athletics an important value in the lives of many people? Who are some of those people? Do you think it might be the only value for some? If so, is this good or bad? Explain.

Was winning a value for Babe Didrikson? Is winning a value for you? Tell what you think is important about winning.

Was practice a value to Babe? What did practice mean in her life? Is practice important to you? Why?

In what ways would you want to be like Babe Didrikson? Why?

Make a list of all the good values you think were part of Babe Didrikson Zaharias.

_____   _____

_____   _____

_____   _____

■BENJAMIN FRANKLIN was born in Boston. His father, a candlemaker, wanted Benjamin to become a minister. When Benjamin was eight, he was sent to school, where he learned quickly. He had already taught himself to read. However, school was costly and the candlemaker was poor, so Ben couldn't continue. As a ten-year-old, he worked in his father's shop.

"I really don't like making candles," he would grumble.

He liked swimming and boating. He wanted to be a sailor, but his father apprenticed Ben to his older brother, James, who was a printer. He went to the print shop when he was twelve. Once again, he learned quickly.

Ben loved to read. He would cut back on what he ate to save money to buy books. He studied mathematics, logic, and navigation. He learned to write by copying newspaper material, rewriting it into poetry, and then changing it back to prose. His skills in composition and grammar advanced quickly.

Ben began submitting articles to his brother's paper under the name "Mrs. Silence Do-good." His brother printed them but became furious when he found out who had written them. Ben, then seventeen, ran away to Philadelphia.

He was hungry. He bought three loaves of bread and walked down the street with one under each arm as he munched on the third. He soon found a job as a printer.

In his life, he was a successful politician, scientist, inventor, author, publisher, philanthropist, businessman, philosopher, statesman, and diplomat. But he always thought of himself as a printer.

Can books be an important value in someone's life? Explain.

Was learning an important value to Benjamin Franklin? What tells you that it was?

What qualities do you admire in Ben Franklin? Why?

In what ways would you want to be like Ben Franklin? Why?

Franklin was successful in many different jobs but always called himself a printer. Why, do you think, did he want to be called a printer?

Make a list of all the good values you think were part of Benjamin Franklin.

_____   _____

_____   _____

_____   _____

■CLARA BARTON was twelve years younger than any of her brothers or sisters. While this made life lonely at times, it did have advantages. Her older sisters became teachers and taught Clara to read. Her brother Stephen, a math teacher, taught her to add and subtract. Her brother David taught her to play ball and ride horses. Clara's father, once a soldier, taught her about history, soldiers, war, and battles. Her mother taught her to cook and sew. There was one thing they could not teach her, however; they could not teach her to stop being shy.

"I don't think I want to go to school," she said. "People I don't know frighten me!" She went, however. She did well in her studies, although she was too shy to talk.

Clara was eleven years old when her father decided to build a new barn. While she watched, a board suddenly broke and her brother David fell to the ground. That night he had a headache and fever. The doctor was very concerned. David would be in bed a long time.

"Let me be his nurse," Clara begged the doctor.

The doctor showed her how to give medicine and to care for him. She was his nurse for months. Finally, David got well.

"My nurse got me well," he told everybody.

Clara had learned that she must help other people. When she began teaching and became ill, her doctor ordered a long rest. She went to Washington to rest, but instead of resting, she took a job in government. When the War Between the States began, there were no nurses to care for the wounded and dying. Wounded soldiers were hauled many miles over rough roads to hospitals.

"Let me go to the battlefields and save men's lives," she pleaded with some of the generals. Finally, they agreed. As a nurse, Clara Barton saved many lives. Later, she went to Europe, where she learned about the Red Cross. When she returned to America, she worked for years to establish the American Red Cross. The shy little girl had grown to be one of the bravest women of all time.

Was helping others a value to Clara Barton? How did it work in her life?

Who benefits when helping others is a value? Explain.

Who had a positive influence on Clara Barton? How?

Who has a positive influence on your life? How?

Would you want to be like Clara? Why or why not?

Make a list of all the good values you think were part of Clara Barton.

_____   _____

_____   _____

_____   _____

■ "THOMAS, what are you doing?" Mrs. Edison asked her curious six-year-old son.

"I'm sitting on some eggs. I saw the goose hatch some, and I want to hatch some, too."

Thomas Alva Edison was always trying things he either read or thought about. At seven years of age, when he went to school, his teacher called him a dunce, so he left school after three months. His mother taught him to love books, however, and he developed a fabulous memory. His father paid him twenty-five cents for each book he read. "I can peddle newspapers, candies, peanuts, and sandwiches on the *Grand Trunk Railway*," he told his parents when he was twelve.

When he visited the Detroit Public Library, the large number of books impressed him. "If I read them all, I'll know all there is to know. I'll read a foot of books every week!"

One night while Edison was selling newspapers at a railroad stop, the train started to pull out. When he seized the handrail on the last car, a brakeman grabbed Tom's ears and pulled him aboard. The yanking on his ear caused deafness.

"I don't mind," Thomas declared. "I can concentrate better."

Before he was fifteen, he set up a printing press in the baggage car. Thomas, by himself, printed a weekly paper, the first one ever on a moving train. Later, he added a lab to the printing press. He ran carefully designed experiments and kept accurate records. When one of the chemicals ignited, the conductor threw Thomas, his printing press, and his lab off the train.

Thomas Edison became a great inventor, making one invention after another until he was a very old man.

If we lose something that is a value to us, do we sometimes replace it with another value? Did Thomas Edison ever do this? Explain.

Was curiosity a value to Edison? How? Is curiosity a value to you? How?

Was knowledge a value to Thomas Edison? Is wanting to know more an important value in your life? Why?

Would you want to be like Edison? Why or why not?

Make a list of all the good values you think were part of Thomas Edison.

_____   _____

_____   _____

_____   _____

■ JOAN was the daughter of a French peasant farmer. As the youngest of five children, she did all the little chores that are the responsibility of farm children. She helped in the house, tended animals, worked on crops — and found time to play. There was no TV, no stereo, no radio, and probably few toys. Like most children of her day, she had to invent toys by borrowing things from nature. At age thirteen, she had a vision.

"There was a voice," she told her family. "Then there was a blaze of light!"

There were other voices that told her to save France. As a peasant teenager, Joan wondered at the messages. After a while, she went to a French military commander. "I've been told to lead France to military victory," she told him. He smiled and tried to send her back home.

"The French will be defeated at Orleans," she predicted. "That's not possible," the commander said. "You're a nice girl. Just go home."

After the French were defeated at Orleans, making the prediction come true, the commander sent Joan to the dauphin, the irresponsible prince of France. "Very well," said the dauphin. "You will lead an expedition to help besieged Orleans."

In a suit of white armor, the teenager from Arc led her forces to victory — and many more after that one. Finally, Joan of Arc was captured and sold to the British. They put her on trial and accused her of heresy and witchcraft. The British burned Joan at the stake, although she was innocent. She was only nineteen, but she had saved France.

Was France (her country) one of Joan of Arc's values? Was courage one of her values? Tell some ways that France and courage influenced Joan's life.

What is there about Joan that makes her a person you might like to imitate?

Could you use any of Joan's values in your life? Which ones? How would you use them?

Joan's family was very poor and there were no modern conveniences. What values do you think were important in her family when she was a young girl?

Make a list of all the good values you think were part of Joan of Arc.

_____   _____

_____   _____

_____   _____

We tend to judge how others act:
Agree or disagree.
We infer from what people do
Their inmost pedigree.

Character Sketches

■ A CHARACTER SKETCH is developed as a result of watching someone's behavior and making note of her attitudes. This sketch or personality profile may be positive, or it may be highly critical. Often, outside values are used by others to form these character sketches. In actions and words, the individual being described communicates her values and the kind of life she wants to live.

When using these character sketches to help kids discover values, don't be too technical. Just suggest that the comments tell us something about the person's values. Keep the discussion from becoming riddled with judgments and sweeping accusations regarding the person's God-created goodness.

A major advantage to this exercise is that it helps kids understand that what they see modeled in another person can help them decide what kind of person they'd like to be. If they can hold the person in positive regard, they have attained a positive model. If they can't hold the person in positive regard, they are better equipped to consider alternative values and behaviors. As part of your discussion, ask the kids, "How would you change this person's behavior to make him or her someone you would like and admire?"

The very fiber of our own self-image is born of how others react to us. When their reactions are positive, our self-image tends to become more positive. When their reactions are negative, our self-image suffers.

What people say about Polly: "Polly uses four little words more than any others: 'How can I help?' She is always doing something for someone."

What does this tell you about one of Polly's values?

How important is it to be helpful? Explain.

Would you like this said about you? Why or why not?

~~~~~~~~~~~~~~~~

What people say about Barry: "Barry is a cheater. Watch him closely!"

How valuable is a good reputation? Explain.

What are some of Barry's values? How do you know?

How would you feel if this was said about you? Why?

What people say about Nan: "I won't believe Nan no matter what she says. I've heard too many lies come out of her mouth!"

Do you think Nan has a value? Is it a good value? Explain.

Would you value Nan as a friend? Why or why not?

Would you like people to talk about you this way? Why or why not?

<div align="center">~~~~~~~~~~~~~~~~</div>

What people say about Evan: "Evan is the most honest boy I've ever met. I'll bet he's never told a lie."

What is Evan's strong value and how do you know this is a value?

What kind of friend do you think Evan would be?

How, do you think, does Evan feel when he hears what people say about him?

What people say about Heather: "I'm sure that the laziest girl I've ever seen anywhere is Heather. She just loafs her life away."

Do loafers have any values? Explain.

Do you think Heather has much to be proud of? Why or why not?

Would you like these comments made about you? Why or why not?

~~~~~~~~~~~~~~~

What people say about Kate: "Isn't Kate a hardworking girl. She helps at home. She studies late every night. She's in extracurricular activities at school. She even carries a paper route."

Does Kate's busy schedule tell us anything about her values? What?

Would Kate be a good friend? Why or why not?

Would you like people to think of you the same way they think of Kate? Why or why not?

What people say about Scott: "Scott is the noisiest boy in the whole city. I mean it. He has to be noisier than anyone else. He has to be!"

Would you want this said about you? Why or why not?

Do you think Scott would be a good friend? Why or why not?

Can you guess one of Scott's values? How could you tell this is one of his values?

~~~~~~~~~~~~~~~~

What people say about Nate: "Nate always listens and tries to understand. He listens carefully to the teacher. Yeah, and he listens to us kids, too."

Do you think listening is important? Why or why not?

Would Nate be a nice person to be around? Explain.

Would you like to be thought of the way people think of Nate? Why or why not?

What people say about Thad: "Such a kind boy. He comes over almost every day to drag my garden hose out and then to drag it back in at night. He climbed the tree to get little Carol's kitten down for her. And Thad is always so polite."

Do you think Thad has values that he lives by? Why or why not?

Do you think Thad likes what people say? Explain.

Is being kind always easy? Explain why or why not.

~~~~~~~~~~~~~~~~

What people say about Leroy: "He's the meanest boy in the neighborhood. He rides his bike across our yards. He abuses our pets. If we say anything, he sasses back."

Try to name just one of Leroy's values.

Would you want Leroy as a friend? Why or why not?

How would you feel if people talked about you as they do Leroy? Explain.

What people say about Cara: "Cara is a curious girl. She's always finding out how something works or why something happens. She just wants to know everything."

Name some of Cara's values.

Would you like to be called curious? Why or why not?

Do you have any curious friends? What are they like?

~~~~~~~~~~~~~~~~

What people say about Edna: "Have you ever known a happier girl? She's always smiling and laughing. She chatters and is so excited. Edna is fun to be near."

Do you like to be around happy people? Why or why not?

Would Edna make a good friend? Explain.

Is happiness a value? Tell why or why not.

What people say about Alice: "I've noticed that, too. For a little girl, she is so very friendly. She speaks to everyone. She waves when we go by. I think she talks to every kid in town."

What are some values that friendly people have?

Is it easy or hard to be friendly? Explain.

Do people call you friendly? Do you agree?

~~~~~~~~~~~~~~~~

What people say about Clayton: "He's always complaining. Nothing is right. How can he be that way?"

What is one value Clayton might have? Explain.

Do complainers make good friends? Why or why not?

Do others think that you complain a lot? Why or why not?

What people say about Russ: "He's a thief. Why, I think he'd steal from his own mother!"

Do you think a thief might have values? Explain.

Name one value you think Russ has. What makes you think this is one of Russ's values?

Would you want to be thought of as a thief? Why or why not?

~~~~~~~~~~~~~~~~

What people say about Vera: "Vera is very responsible. She does what she is expected to do and she does it well. You can always depend on Vera to do what's right."

What one value might Vera have? How can you tell?

Are you responsible? Do others think so? How can you tell?

Would you like being called responsible? Why or why not?

What people say about Bonnie: "She really isn't funny. Bonnie keeps making smart remarks about people. She thinks she has a right to tease and torment others. Then she laughs at their unhappiness."

Do you know a person who is like Bonnie? Tell about that person.

Do you think that people who are like Bonnie are happy? Why or why not?

What might one of Bonnie's values be? Explain.

~~~~~~~~~~~~~~~

What people say about Lisa: "I wish Lisa would just leave me alone. I don't like her playing jokes on me. She could be nice, but she has to be a joker."

Why do people play jokes on others?

Would you like to be known as a joker? Why or why not?

People who play jokes hurt others. Are their values good or bad? Explain.

Mr. Jones is an excellent teacher.
Guessed we were tired and bored.
He gave us a grin and a smile and a laugh
Our attention was quickly restored.

Limericks

■ LIMERICKS provide a fun way to approach the process of helping kids discover values. The limerick is a light five-line rhyme that is loaded with values. Words are a crucial component of these exercises and some have been altered to accommodate the rhyme. Be sure every youngster grasps the meaning of each word in the limerick.

Keep in mind the two types of values discussed in the introduction: the inside value (motivator) and the outside value (communicator). Through the inside value, we perceive something as good and worth acquiring. Through the outside value, we tell others how we want to live.

We act out our values and experience rewards and costs as a result of our behavior. Ideally, we would like youngsters to recognize both rewards and costs as early as possible. Such recognition requires appropriate levels of maturation. Our primary objective here is to help kids discover values.

The younger the child, the more difficult it may be for him or her to identify and respond to values within the stimulus situation. We may need to provide more cue questions and offer more individual attention.

There once was a bothersome lass
Who could have been first in her class.
But she walked, talked, and played,
and her teacher dismayed.
She barely was able to pass.

Was the lass's behavior good or bad? In what way?

What does this lass need to correct?

Is her behavior worth the cost to her?

If you were this lass, what would your ambitions be? Why?

There once was a talented lass,
Who worked hard and tried hard to pass.
Her friends cheered aloud,
and her parents were proud
Of the honors she won in her class.

Compare the lass in this limerick with the one in the limerick at the top of the page.

There once was a cocky young male
Who bragged that he just couldn't fail
  To slyly shoplift
  A much-wanted gift.
Now he's doing his bragging in jail.

How was the young man in this limerick stupid?

Do you think he thought he was stupid? Explain.

How will he have to change to be smart?

Why is it wrong to take what belongs to someone else?

Bobby made toys out of wood,
And everyone said they were good.
  Kids came to eye 'em,
  Some came to buy 'em.
With the money he bought what he could.

Compare Bobby in this limerick with the cocky
young male in the limerick at the top of the page.

A small woman sat in a chair
And none of her riches would share.
   Before she could holler
   Thugs took every dollar.
Now she's begging to ease her despair.

Why is it important to share?

How do you feel when someone shares with you?

How do you feel when you share with others?

Should you help someone who never shares? Why or why not?

A very nice lady from Maine
Had nothing at all to her name.
   Had little to eat
   But shared all her meat.
To share was her heart's loving aim.

Compare the lady in this limerick with the small woman in the limerick at the top of the page.

There once was a thoughtless young lass
Who threw rocks at all window glass.
   She broke more than a few,
   Some were old, some were new,
She gained no respect in her class.

Why is it important to respect other people's property?

Why do people want to destroy or damage other people's property?

What is the crime of vandalism?

What does this limerick say about vandalism?

There was a pretty young daughter
Who skipped many pebbles on water.
   She ne'er hurt anyone,
   She was just wanting fun
And fun is just what it all got her!

Compare the young daughter in this limerick with the lass in the limerick at the top of the page.

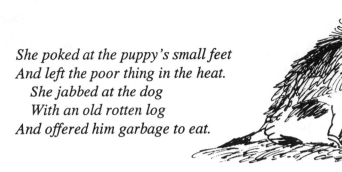

She poked at the puppy's small feet
And left the poor thing in the heat.
She jabbed at the dog
With an old rotten log
And offered him garbage to eat.

What is wrong with abusing animals?

If you treat animals kindly, how will they probably treat you?

How would you feel and what would you do if you saw someone abusing an animal?

What are some good reasons for loving and respecting all forms of life?

A thirsty cat stood near the trail
And lapped up milk from a pail.
A girl standing by
Gave kitty a "Hi,"
And the cat gave a swish of her tail.

Compare what happens in this limerick with what happens in the one at the top of the page.

There once was a naughty young daughter,
Who did things she just shouldn't ought'er.
   For good things she was thanked,
   And for bad things she was spanked.
She finally learned what being good got her.

Have you ever had experiences like this girl? Explain.

What does being good get you? What does being bad cost you?

Can you be good all the time? Why or why not?

Is it all right for you to "mess up" once in a while when you're really trying to be good? Why or why not?

A happy, obedient maid
Was as sweet as pink lemonade.
   The sad she consoled.
   Did what she was told.
Good behavior she put on parade!

Compare the maid in this limerick with the daughter in the limerick at the top of the page.

Over there is a splendid young man
Who behaves as well as he can.
*   For by acting that way*
*   He gets praise every day.*
His actions seem right by this plan.

Why is it important to please
our families and friends?

Are there times when pleasing someone else might not be the best thing
to do? Give an example.

How does praise make you feel?

Can you and should you be praised for negative behavior such as lying?
Why or why not?

Over there is a discourteous bloke
Who acts as if life is a joke.
*   He cares not for others,*
*   Cheats his sisters and brothers*
And steals from all neighboring folk.

Compare the person in this limerick
with the person in the limerick
at the top of the page.

There once was a person so bold,
He never did what he was told.
  He would not obey,
    Had to have his own way.
Now from prison he may be paroled.

Was this person's behavior good or bad? How?

What does this person need to correct? Why?

What does this person's behavior cost him? Is it worth the cost?

If you were a friend of this person, what would you help him learn? How and why?

There once was an honorable man
Who lived by an unselfish plan.
  Cared for the helpless he saw,
    Valued all points of the law.
He was honored as best in his clan.

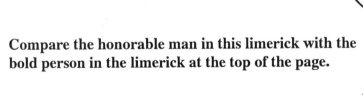

Compare the honorable man in this limerick with the bold person in the limerick at the top of the page.

There was a frisky young pup
Who decided to drink from a cup.
*   He gulped beer from a mug*
*   And whiskey from a jug.*
Now his friends have to help him stand up.

Do you approve of what the pup did? Why or why not?

What was good or bad about the pup's behavior?

Do people sometimes act like the pup? Give examples.

How does "Just say no" relate to this limerick?

There once was a lifeless old dog
Who tried to jump over a log.
*   He stubbed all his toes,*
*   landed flat on his nose.*
Next morning he started to jog.

Compare the dog in this limerick with the pup in the limerick at the top of the page.

The good you do
And the good I see
May be different things
Within you and me.

Fables

■ FABLES are to be read with or to a group of young people, followed with an opportunity for discussion. After each fable presented here, a short list of questions is provided to help get the discussion started.

Each fable offers a concluding moral. Help the youngsters understand the meaning of each moral and how it is demonstrated in the story. From there you can draw the kids into looking at their own lives to see if they deal with any of the same moral issues.

Fables usually feature animal characters with human traits and abilities. One helpful discussion approach is to look for the human strengths and weaknesses in each animal. The strengths and weaknesses often parallel nicely with the internal and external values that a human being might display.

Remember, we are trying to help kids discover their inside values. These internal values are something good that kids see and then set out to live. They begin to realize that living a particular value is often at a tremendous cost. If we can help kids discover these inside values, we're better equipped to help them minimize the costs. Since some values are bad or negative, and often come with a high cost to the individual, it is worth pursuing questions and discussions that give young people opportunities to look at internal values in light of cost. Fables offer one vehicle for this: the moral is often stated in terms of cost.

Fables provide discussion pieces for young and old alike to identify elements of right and wrong in the behavior of the animal creatures taking on human characteristics. We project these judgments of right and wrong from the growing and changing system "inside" ourselves.

■A LARGE DOG had been his master's only companion for several years. One day, the master adopted a stray kitten and then left the dog and the kitten alone in the house while he went on a trip. While he was gone, it became bitter cold and the house got colder and colder.

"I'm cold," whimpered the kitten.

"So why tell me?" snapped the dog. "I'm not here to worry about you."

"Can I sleep in your bed with you?" coaxed the kitten. She tried to climb into the dog's bed with him, but the dog prized his box with its old blankets.

"You're not a puppy," he growled as he pushed the kitten out.

"I know I'm not a puppy, but I'm still cold," the kitten whined.

For a moment, the dog watched his companion shiver. "Okay, get in here but be quiet!" the dog ordered.

After a while, the dog realized that he was warmer with the kitten cuddled up against him.

"This was a good idea," he said.

MORAL: Sharing is not all giving.

The moral of a fable is meant to tell us something important about how human beings behave. What does the moral of this fable suggest to us about life?

Some fables give us more than one moral. Can you discover another moral in this fable?

If the dog had remained selfish and had not shared his bed with the kitten, would the fable have a moral? Explain.

What might we add to the fable that would give the moral greater meaning?

■ IN THE SPRING, all the eggs had been hatched and there were many baby chicks scurrying about. The farmer worked hard to take care of his flock.

One little hen was noticed by all in the barnyard. Each day she grew a little and each day her voice became louder. Before she was very old, she had the loudest voice in the chicken pen.

"What a loud mouth you have," teased one young rooster. He was jealous because the little hen could squawk much louder than he could.

Every day the little hen was teased more and more about her loud voice. Gradually, she became sad because she was so different from the rest of the little hens. "Please don't tease me," she whispered, but even her whisper was loud. All the other hens laughed — and that's the way the little hen grew up.

One night the fox came. Just as he was about to grab one of the hens and some eggs, the hen with the loud voice screamed as loud as she could. Her scream awakened the farmer's big watchdog, who came running to scare away the fox. The hen with the loud voice had saved the henhouse and all the hens clucked, "Thank you."

MORAL: All of us are made to play a special role.

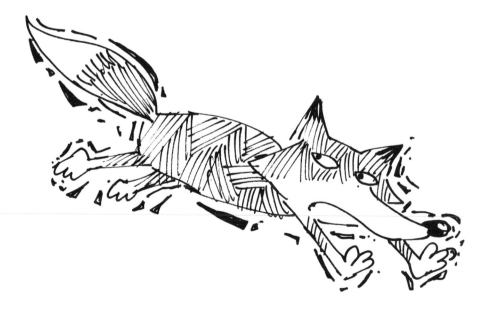

The moral of a fable is meant to tell us something important about how human beings behave. What does the moral of this fable suggest about life?

What important message does this moral give us about human differences?

Some fables give us more than one moral. Can you discover another moral in this fable?

Is there anything wrong with being different? Imagine that all human beings were exactly alike. Would you prefer that to being different? Explain.

THE NEIGHBORHOOD DOG was a bully. Anytime the cat or the squirrel scampered near, the dog would chase it viciously. One day the cat escaped by climbing a tree. She found the squirrel on one of the branches. "That was close," the cat panted.

"I know," said the squirrel. "I can't even go dig in the snow for food. I'm getting very weak."

"And I can't go in my yard," added the cat.

The two looked down at the dog, who waited below.

"You must be getting hungry," the cat observed.

"Oh, I am," the squirrel agreed.

"My master has walnuts in a bowl for his holiday guests. I could get you one, but the dog might get me," meowed the cat.

"I can distract the dog for you," offered the squirrel. "Watch."

She then turned and abruptly jumped to the next tree — and then the next and the next. From below, the dog saw the squirrel and started to follow it — which left the yard below unguarded. The cat scampered down the tree, ran cautiously to the house, grabbed a walnut, dashed back to the tree, and scurried up the trunk.

The cat gave the walnut to the squirrel when she returned. "I'll help you and you help me," suggested the squirrel. "We'll beat that dog!"

MORAL: Cooperation brings many victories.

The moral of a fable is meant to tell us something important about how human beings behave. What does the moral of this fable suggest about life?

Some fables give us more than one moral. Can you discover another moral in this fable?

The cat and the squirrel cooperated. If they had been competing, what might have happened to them? How would you apply this to your own life?

What might we add to the fable that would give the moral greater meaning?

■ AS HE HAD DONE many times before, the eagle swooped down to catch the rabbit. The rabbit escaped but not by much. The eagle screamed across the valley, "I'll get you yet!"

From his hiding place near the boulder, the rabbit watched with fear as the bobcat strolled down to drink from the stream. The rabbit knew the cat's pattern: after his drink, he would roam back up the hill, sniff around the boulder, and wiggle through the hollow log. "I'm in terrible trouble," trembled the rabbit. "If I stay here, the bobcat might get me; if I don't stay here, the eagle might get me."

While he watched the bobcat drinking and the eagle soaring above, the rabbit came up with a plan. He ran through the open and jumped into the log right behind the bobcat as he entered on his way up from the stream. The eagle saw the rabbit and began his dive. Seeing the rabbit enter the log, he circled quickly and sprang on the bobcat — which he had expected to be a rabbit — as it came out the other end. The bobcat clawed at the eagle, leaving a deep scratch on the eagle's leg.

The eagle quickly retreated. "I'll hunt elsewhere," he said, "where rabbits aren't so tough."

As the bobcat ran away, he, too, made a decision: "I'm going to live someplace else — someplace where eagles don't attack bobcats."

MORAL: Courage and clear thinking always solve the problem.

The moral of a fable is meant to tell us something important about how human beings behave. What does the moral of this fable suggest about life?

How do you apply this moral to what you do from day to day?

What mistakes did the rabbit cause the eagle and the bobcat to make? How did these mistakes change the lives of all three animals?

What might have happened to the rabbit if his trick did not work? What does this tell us about the importance of learning to think clearly?

■ THE DEER and the beaver met every morning. The deer sipped cool water from the stream while the beaver chiseled away at a tree.

"Why do you keep chewing up trees?" asked the deer.

The beaver sat up for a minute and smacked his lips. "Partly, I eat trees," he said. "Really, I'm building a dam to make the water deeper."

The deer took another cool sip. "Why?" he asked.

Again the beaver stopped working on the tree. "Because then I can build a lodge," explained the beaver.

"I'm sorry to be so curious," said the deer, "but why do you need a lodge?"

"For protection against my enemies and to keep me warm in the winter."

The deer shook his antlers. "I just run from my enemies," he told the beaver.

"Exactly, but I can't run as fast as you can. I have to plan and work to survive."

MORAL: Preparation and anticipation make for a longer life.

The moral of a fable is meant to tell us something important about how human beings behave. What does the moral of this fable suggest about life?

Is it possible for any of us to imitate the beaver? How can we plan and work to make our lives better?

Some fables give us more than one moral. Can you discover another moral in this fable?

The deer came to the water to drink. The beaver came to the water to change it, to make it deeper, to live in it. What does the behavior of the deer and the behavior of the beaver show us about human behavior?

A HUNGRY TIGER walked under a branch on which a peacock perched. The tiger planned to flatter the bird into coming down from the branch so he could grab the peacock and eat it for dinner. The tiger looked up with a big smile on his face.

"Good morning," the big cat said. "You're such a beautiful bird!"

Seeing the cat's smile, the peacock bowed and fanned his feathers.

"Not compared to you, you handsome fellow," the bird said. "Your striped coat is brilliant."

The tiger considered the statement thoughtfully. "Hmm, you're right. I do have a stunning coat."

"Yes, and a striking profile, too. And such a muscular body. And a most interesting face. And such sparkling eyes. And the most powerful jaws I have ever admired. And you walk with such grace. And you stand with such poise."

The tiger shook his head in agreement. "I came here to eat you," he told the bird. "But your words are so much more filling than you would be. I won't bother."

The tiger then strutted off proudly.

MORAL: Kind words are never wasted.

The moral of a fable is meant to tell us something important about how human beings behave. What does the moral of this fable suggest about life?

Some fables give us more than one moral. Can you discover another moral in this fable?

What might have happened if the peacock had just accepted the tiger's flattery? Would there be a moral?

Do you think the peacock might have laughed at the tiger after the tiger left? Why? Should we laugh when we get the best of someone?

■ A YOUNG ELK, his antlers held high, stood with an old stag at the edge of the forest. Down below there spread a lush meadow where the tall, thick, deep green grass swayed in the gentle breeze. "I think I'll walk down and feast on that grass," said the young elk.

The old stag snorted and pawed the ground. "Let me give you some advice: don't do it."

The eyes of the young elk glimmered in the sun as he scanned the meadow. "Why not?" he asked. "The grass is thick and green and covered with dew. I've never had a chance like this."

The old elk moved closer to his young companion. "Listen to me carefully," he cautioned. "The hunters are out today. Don't go out in the open."

The young elk stood for a long time staring at the grass and thinking about the stag's warning. Finally, he ignored his elder and slowly walked down the hill. When he reached the beautiful grass, he began to enjoy its moist taste.

Up above, at the edge of the forest, the old-timer waited and watched. He stomped uneasily on the ground — and a moment later a shot was heard. The old elk looked sadly below, shook his head, and slipped deep into the protection of the woods.

MORAL: Even free advice can be valuable.

The moral of a fable is meant to tell us something important about how human beings behave. What does the moral of this fable suggest about life?

The moral mentions "free advice." What is free advice and when might it be wise to follow it?

What are examples of advice that is not free? Is it important to follow advice that is not free? Explain.

Some fables give us more than one moral. Can you discover another moral in this fable?

■ A FLOCK of small brown birds soared above the herd of antelope. A short time later, they perched on the backs of the antelopes, who seemed to expect them. One bird sat on the neck of an antelope, not far from her ear. "And how is my favorite antelope today?" he asked.

The antelope raised her head and moaned softly. "Not well. Not well at all," she answered. "The insects are biting my back."

The little bird offered some words of encouragement as he hopped down onto the back of his friend. "I see what you mean. I'll take care of that for you," he promised.

Immediately, the bird began eating the insects, and the antelope went back to grazing on the field grass. It didn't take long for the bird to remove many insects. He gave a little burp. "They make a fine dinner," he remarked. "Thank you!"

The antelope stretched and smiled. "And I'm feeling much better," she declared. "Thank you!"

A short time later, the birds sensed the approach of a lion and began to give shrill cries. Immediately, the antelopes ran to safety with the birds on their backs.

MORAL: One good deed deserves another.

The moral of a fable is meant to tell us something important about how human beings behave. What does the moral of this fable suggest about life?

Explain how you can apply the meaning of this moral in your own life.

Some fables give us more than one moral. Can you discover another moral in this fable?

The moral uses the term "good deed." What are some good deeds we see in the fable?

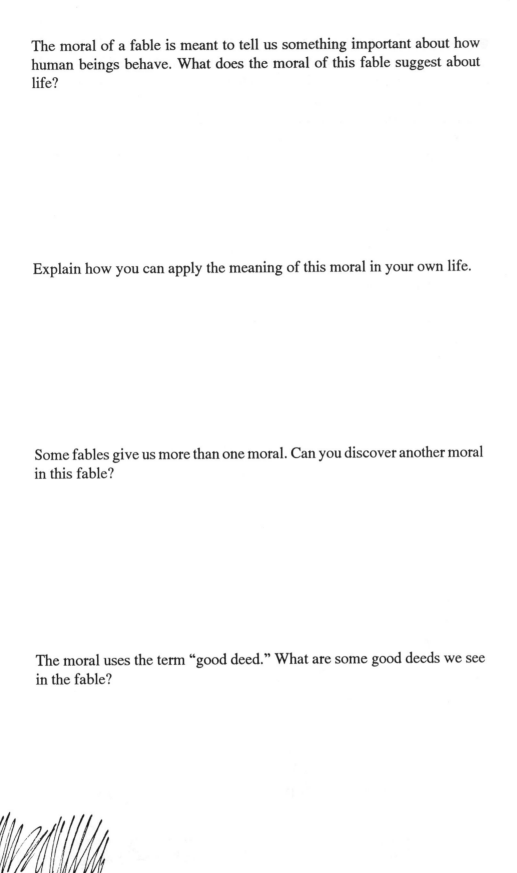

■A BRIGHTLY COLORED ROOSTER walked majestically up and down the rows of garden plants, eating one insect after another. He looked carefully under the leaves and along all the stems and around the flowers.

"Wait!" hollered one little bug. "Don't eat me before we talk."

The rooster looked sternly at the insect. "Talk?" he asked. "Talk about what?"

The insect gulped hard before he answered. "You're making a big mistake. You should eat the peas or the beans or the fruit instead of us poor little fellows. The fruit would be much more filling."

"Well, I guess you're right," the rooster agreed. "But the fruit belongs to my master, and I'm very loyal."

"You must reconsider," pleaded the little bug.

"There is nothing to reconsider," the rooster insisted.

"Oh, a big fine rooster like you needs to eat well — and we bugs are so small," the insect continued.

"No! I'm here to protect my master's plants from little thieves like you," said the rooster. "That's my job, and I must do it."

And with that, he ate the insect.

MORAL: It is difficult to delay what must happen.

The moral of a fable is meant to tell us something important about how human beings behave. What does the moral of this fable suggest about life?

Some fables give us more than one moral. Can you discover another moral in this fable?

Are insects less important than roosters and, therefore, roosters can eat insects? Are roosters less important than people and, therefore, people can eat roosters? What do you think? Explain.

Does the rooster respect his master? Is he loyal to him? How do we know? Is this as it should be?

■ THE ANIMALS gathered in the barnyard to boast to one another about their individual virtues.

"I can honk quite loud," the goose declared.

"Yes, I know," agreed the turkey. "But I have a fine voice, too — and I can even gobble."

The pig gave a satisfied grunt. "I can eat more and faster than any one of you," he bragged.

"I can carry our owner on my back," the horse pointed out. "I'm the only one who can do that."

"That's true," groaned the cow. "But I'm the only one who provides our owner with milk."

"Aah, but I produce down for the owner's pillow," honked the goose.

"True, but I dispose of all the owner's slop," grunted the pig.

"Yes, of course. I'm the only one here, though, who can chew her cud," claimed the cow.

"I can run faster than any of you," snorted the horse.

The turkey gave them all a sly little smile. "In the end," he promised, "I shall be the center of the owner's holiday celebration."

MORAL: Everyone wants to be good at something.

The moral of a fable is meant to tell us something important about how human beings behave. What does the moral of this fable suggest about life?

Some fables give us more than one moral. Can you discover another moral in this fable?

The turkey seems to know that he has a very special role to play. Do we each have special roles in our lives? What is a special role you play in your life?

The characters in this fable know what's special and different about themselves. Do we have any responsibilities that are uniquely ours because we're human beings? Explain one.

The poet sends a message
For the reader to receive,
While the reader keeps an open eye
As to what he will perceive.

Poems

■ THESE POEMS reflect values that dramatize the good in behavior and in environment. Keep the following guidelines in mind when leading a discussion:

- Involve every youngster in evaluating what is good, what is right, and what is beautiful in the poem.
- Try to keep channels open for youngsters' individual meanings and interpretations.
- Use the questions at the end of each poem to keep the discussion moving. Allow plenty of flexibility as the discussion develops.
- Watch for "I don't know" reactions, shrugs instead of answers, expressions of puzzlement or shyness, and no answers at all. These may indicate that the youngster is not understanding the words or the theme of the poem.
- Ask questions about what words mean or what some lines are saying. Talk about any tough words or ideas. Help the youngsters get the basic ideas so they can look for value ideas.

You might ask the young people, "What does the poem say to you?" Remember: all responses are acceptable. Discoveries can evolve out of any reasonable exchange.

POEMS

Home and Family

A furry little beaver
Was chomping on the wood,
Dropping down the forest trees
Anywhere he could.
He was piling logs and branches
To make a sturdy dam.
"I'm building me a house," he said.
"I am, I am, I am!"

A husky, sweaty carpenter
Pounded with a thud,
Nailing tight the two-by-fours
To make each upright stud.
Then adding sheathing for the walls,
A window for some light —
"I'm building me a house," he said.
"All right, all right, all right!"

Be it man or animal,
His home is still his dream.
Running water from the tap
Or from the running stream.
Each finishing the house inside
To fill his every need
For a living, loving family —
Indeed, indeed, indeed!

Is home important to the beaver? Why does the beaver work so hard?

Is home important to the carpenter? Why does the carpenter work so hard?

Does the beaver love his family? Does the carpenter love his family? Why is love so important?

The beaver is created by God. The carpenter is created by God. How are they alike? How are they different?

Who has greater control over the world, the beaver or the man? Who has the greater responsibility?

Do we have responsibilities toward the animals? If so, what are those responsibilities?

Friendship

Bingo was a lively pup
living on a farm.
He trailed behind his mother
Who shielded him from harm.
He was a very nosy beast
With curiosity galore —
And seven hundred acres
Is a big place to explore.

Inside the huge white farmhouse
There was a little boy
Who was grown up enough, you see,
Those acres to enjoy.
He loved to roam the cabbage patch
And check the melon field,
Collecting worms and spiders
Into bottles to be sealed.

This little boy named Jody
Went walking one bright morn,
And he glimpsed the playful puppy
Chasing crickets by the corn.
Because God made them for each other,
They came together fast.
Boy and dog became great friends,
A friendship that would last.

Have you ever had a pet? Were you and your pet close friends? Tell about this.

What do you think Jody can give Bingo? What do you think Bingo can give Jody?

Can pets keep us from being lonely? If yes, how? If no, why not?

How does exploring the big farm help Bingo? How does exploring the big farm help Jody?

How can Jody and Bingo play and grow together? Will they be good for each other? Explain.

Being Organized

In a quaint stucco house
Lived a smug little bird
And a big hungry cat
Who meowed every word.
The lady who owned them,
In her doddering age,
Fed not the cat
And closed not the cage.

The big hungry cat
Leaped for a kill
As the smug little bird
Jumped off of the sill.
Outside the window
Came a terrible crash.
The cat had jumped out
Right into the trash.

The lady who listened
In her own mixed-up way
While shaking a finger
Was soon heard to say:
"You smug little bird,
Now don't stare like that!
You look like the canary
That swallowed the cat."

Is being organized a value? Why or why not?

Have you ever been disorganized? What happened? Was what happened mostly good or mostly bad? Explain.

Do people sometimes become disorganized? Can we help them? How?

How and why is the lady in the poem disorganized? Is it mostly good or mostly bad?

How might you become more organized in your life?

How do you feel when the canary outguesses the cat? Do you like it when a little fellow (the canary) outwits a big fellow (the cat)? Why do you like or dislike such situations?

Rules

The dwarf was a tiny fellow,
Just fifty pounds he weighed.
His cunning sense of humor
Saved many an escapade.
He lived in a flowery glen,
In a house of wood and stone.
And for his fine woodcarvings
He was loved and widely known.

The giant was a miner.
He weighed four hundred pounds.
He worked deep in the earth all day
Where treasured gold abounds.
He lived above a little store
Along a dusty street.
And sometimes dwarf and giant met
At their favorite place to eat.

Once teasing led to betting,
And the giant made the call.
"We see who lifts the greatest weight,
With most pounds winning all!"
"But I insist on just one rule,"
The dwarf barked with a grin.
"We have to lift twice our own weight
For either man to win."

Would the dwarf or the giant be a better friend to have? Why?

What does the dwarf's rule mean in the contest? Is it a fair rule? Why or why not?

Does the dwarf work? What does he do? Is his work good for him? How?

The giant is a miner. Is his work good for him? How?

What good traits does each man have? What bad traits does each have? How do you recognize these good and bad traits?

Which man would you rather be like? Why?

Differences

She ran and ran and ran and ran
Until out of breath and tired,
She dropped to sit upon a rock,
Feeling happily inspired.
She sat there resting but alert,
Looking all around.
Watching, listening, longing
For God's pictures and God's sound.

He walked slowly, deeply attentive
To each flower's unique shape.
He saw the silent garter snake
As it dashed for an escape.
He froze in place and held his breath
As a rabbit, gray and brown,
Sat nibbling at some leafy plant
And dared to stare him down.

Both boy and girl had seen the awe
And beauty of that place.
She had raced with pounding speed,
But he had slowed his pace.
Did one get more enjoyment?
That clearly seems not so.
Both had seen God gifts of life;
Both claimed a chance to grow!

How is the girl's behavior different from the boy's? Did both learn? If so, how? If not, why not?

Do we have to be different from others? How? Why? Do we have to be like others? How? Why?

Should we always accept the differences we see in other people or are there times when we should refuse to accept differences? Explain.

The boy and girl had their special ways of dealing with life. Do you think each of us needs our own special patterns? Explain.

Wisdom

In the shade of an old oak tree
Stood a bench for those passing by.
Atop a branch high in the tree
An owl kept a watchful eye.
Along the walk came a dear old man
With his cane and his slow-moving pace.
With careful steps and a quiet smile,
He took his usual place.

The bird above watched the man below
As he stretched out his big, tired feet.
The owl left the branch and swept through the air
To perch on the back of the seat.
With a blink of his eyes, he waited awhile
For the talk he knew they'd renew
On the knotty problems of the universe
And solutions that they might pursue.

The old man spilled some grain on the bench,
And the bird hopped quickly to eat.
The man reported the news of the day
While the bird enjoyed his treat.
When the dear man declared what they both ought to try,
The owl gave way with a "Whooo?"
The old man laughed and whispered back,
"There's only me and youuuuu!"

The man has a smile on his face as he sits down on the bench. When we get old, is there a value in being able to go where we want on our own? Explain.

Do you think the old man and the owl have something in common? What might that be?

Is the owl really interested in hearing all the news of the day? Is the owl a good listener? Is the owl mainly interested in eating? What do you think and why?

Is the old man lonely? Is being able to talk to someone a value?

Is it wise to listen to those much older than ourselves? Who gains when we listen to them?

Thieves

Watching slyly from atop the tree
A blue jay viewed the sight.
A picnic table far below
stood spread with fine delight.
"If in my forest you must camp,
My privacy you steal.
And you should simply pay the price:
I'm entitled to your meal."

Slouched low behind the steering wheel
The thief surveyed the scene.
"I have very little money…
I have none is what I mean.
The bank is full of money, though,
Folks drop it off all day.
Since they just leave it sitting 'round,
I'll just take what I may."

Each thief believed to have the right
To take what's near at hand.
We chuckle at the blue jay's view,
But reject what the robber had planned.
It's time to weigh the justice now:
Have two wrongs here occurred?
Can't we expect more from a human
Than we can ever expect from a bird?

Why can we laugh at the feathered thief when we're outwitted at our campsite?

Why are we angry with the bank robber for taking money from a bank?

Can we accept the explanation the blue jay gives to justify taking a meal?

Why do we reject the bank robber's explanation for taking other people's money?

The poem says that we expect more from the human being than from the bird. What does this mean to you?

Freedom

The tiger paced about his cage
And dreamed of roaming free,
Of prancing through the jungle wilds
To see what he could see.
He'd hunt and run and roar and rest
And have things just his way.
But freedom comes at no small cost;
There always a price to pay.

If he could leave his cage behind
And dash out on his own,
Would he be able to accept
A world he's never known?
He sees himself a prisoner now,
Held captive in that place.
But Mr. Tiger doesn't know
What he would really face.

He now enjoys respect from all.
At the zoo he's a major star.
If, in fact, he ran outside,
Would his coat some hunter scar?
In watching you, my tiger friend,
I see it isn't strange
To overlook the way we live
With no regard to change.

What are some of the advantages Mr. Tiger has to being in the zoo? Are there disadvantages?

In our life, do we have a "pretty good deal"? Would we get rid of disadvantages if we were turned out to run "free," or would we have even more disadvantages?

When we do have a "pretty good deal," do we usually hang on to it and not look for something better? Why or why not?

Does the tiger enjoy any freedom in his cage? Explain.

Do we enjoy a fair amount of freedom, even though we have rules and laws to obey? Explain.

When we see something happen,
There are values to be guessed.
Before we counter by some action,
We choose values that are best.

Scenarios

■ A SCENARIO is a sequence of events. The following scenarios present situations that will be familiar to the youngsters.

Each exercise is presented in three sections. The first section presents the scenario: "What You See." A scene is described in which the youngsters are to place themselves.

This brief description is followed by a list of possible actions one might choose to take: "What You Do." Each option should be discussed with the youngsters. "What's good about this action?" "What's wrong?" "What does this action say to others?" "What inside values can be guessed from the action?"

After discussing each of the options listed in "What You Do," ask the youngsters if some other action might be chosen. Allow sufficient time to discuss all alternatives. Then help the youngsters decide which action is best. Ask them to justify their choice.

The third section asks the youngsters to tell what their parent(s) would probably want them to do: "What Your Mom or Dad Would Want You to Do." This offers opportunity for exchange among the youngsters themselves. Some youngsters may realize that their mother would want them to respond in one way while their father would want them to respond in a different way. Do not judge what the youngsters say about their parents. Encourage this exchange in a positive and supportive manner.

Identifying values and using values in our actions are skills. It is the responsibility of adults to provide circumstances in which young people have an opportunity to practice these skills.

What You See

You're walking along the sidewalk. Across the street, a small girl is playing with a cute puppy, and you stop to watch. You decide to walk over and ask her if you can pet her puppy. As you step from the curb, however, you see a car coming fast. You wait for it to pass, but the puppy doesn't. He runs into the street and the car hits him, throwing him near the curb on the other side of the street. The small girl runs to her puppy who squirms twice and then is very still. She stands there with her hands extended, then begins to cry as if her heart is breaking.

What You Do

☐ You go to the girl and tell her not to cry.
☐ You go to the girl, ask her where she lives, and take her and her puppy there.
☐ You stand by the puppy and tell the girl to get one of her parents.
☐ You tell the girl her puppy is dead and offer to help her find another one.
☐ You feel sad, so you just turn away and keep walking.
☐ You do something else. What?

What Your Mom or Dad Would Want You to Do

Tell what this might be.

What You See

You've just come out of the supermarket, where you bought a candy bar. You stand on the sidewalk and begin eating it. As you watch people go in and come out, you see one lady with a big sack of groceries. When she tries to shift the sack from one arm to the other, it splits open. Items spill out, causing her to drop the bag completely. Her purchases scatter all over the ground.

What You Do

☐ You laugh at how funny the groceries look rolling about on the pavement.

☐ You begin picking up things and handing them to the lady.

☐ You run into the store, tell a checker what happened, get a new sack, and return to help the lady pick up everything.

☐ You grab a nearby empty grocery cart, push it to the lady, and ask her how you can help.

☐ You walk away, telling yourself that it's none of your business.

☐ You do something else. What?

What Your Mom or Dad Would Want You to Do

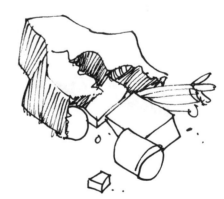

Tell what this might be.

What You See

You start to ride your bike home from school. It snowed while you were in school, and everything is very slick. As you attempt to make a turn, the wheels skid and you go down. You get a couple bumps, but you're really not hurt. You decide to just walk your bike home, though. Along the way, you notice an old man walking very slowly. He's using a cane. You look away to check the street before crossing. You hear a moan. When you look back, the old man is on the ground.

What You Do

☐ You lay your bike down and run to help the man.
☐ You call to the man and ask if he is all right.
☐ You stand and wait to see if the man can get up by himself.
☐ You walk your bike toward the man, watching to see what he does.
☐ The man is a stranger, so you just walk away.
☐ You do something else. What?

What Your Mom or Dad Would Want You to Do

Tell what this might be.

What You See

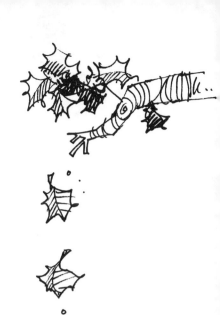

While riding your bike around the neighborhood, you notice a boy about four years old. He's trying to climb a large tree. You slow down to watch him struggle up the trunk to grab the first branch. Finally, he pulls himself up to where he is about ten feet off the ground. As he wiggles around to get his foot on the next branch, he slips and falls, headfirst, to the ground.

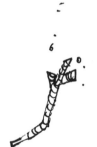

What You Do

☐ You run to the nearest house to ask for help.
☐ You go to the boy to help him up.
☐ You run to where the boy is and yell "Help" over and over as loud as you can.
☐ You find the first adult you can and ask for help.
☐ You just say, "Dumb kid," and ride away.
☐ You do something else. What?

What Your Mom or Dad Would Want You to Do

Tell what this might be.

What You See

Your mother has sent you to the supermarket to pick up milk and eggs. On your way home, you notice an elderly lady using a walker. She is standing beneath a tree, looking up, and shaking her finger at something. You look closer. There on one of the upper limbs is a kitten. "You come down, Kitty! Do you hear me?" the lady is saying over and over. The kitten, too frightened to come down, simply answers, "Meow."

What You Do

☐ You talk to the lady and suggest that she call the fire department.
☐ You put your milk and eggs on the ground and climb up to bring the kitten down.
☐ You ask the lady if she has thought of spraying the kitten with her garden hose.
☐ You suggest to the lady that she sit on her porch for a while and the kitten will come down.
☐ You don't stop at all. You hurry home to get the groceries to your mother.
☐ You do something else. What?

What Your Mom or Dad Would Want You to Do

Tell what this might be.

What You See

You're standing at a busy corner waiting for the red light to turn green so you can safely cross the street. Two vehicles suddenly smash together in the middle of the intersection. The sedan rolls over on its side and slides; the pickup goes out of control and slams into a utility pole. The pickup, going the same direction that you were waiting to go, had gone through the red light.

What You Do

☐ You see several adults running toward the vehicles, and you run with them.

☐ You see several adults running toward the vehicles, but you wait and watch from the sidewalk.

☐ You run into the nearby store and tell the clerk to call the police.

☐ You watch until police cars arrive. Then you explain to an officer that you're sure the pickup ran the red light.

☐ You don't wait. You just hurry along to wherever you were going.

☐ You do something else. What?

What Your Mom or Dad Would Want You to Do

Tell what this might be.

What You See

You usually arrive home from school about four p.m. One afternoon, you get there to find your mother in bed. "Better stay away from me," she says. "I think I have the flu." She tells you she has taken some medicine and will stay in bed to see if it helps her. You know that means she won't be able to cook supper. As you look around, it's obvious that she's been ill all day. None of her usual chores are done.

What You Do

☐ You call the family doctor, tell him the situation, and ask what you should do for your mother.
☐ You begin doing your mother's chores.
☐ You turn the TV on with the sound very low and let your mother rest.
☐ You get a chair and sit by your mother's bedroom door so you can get her anything she wants.
☐ You fix a peanut-butter sandwich and go out to play.
☐ You do something else. What?

What Your Mom or Dad Would Want You to Do

Tell what this might be.

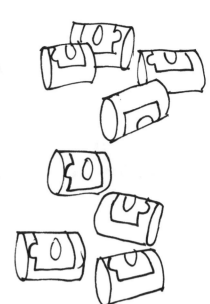

What You See

You're in the supermarket looking for a notebook to use in school. Near the shelves of school supplies is a canned-goods display. Hundreds of cans are stacked in a circle. While you look through the shelves to find the kind of notebook you need, you back up a little too far. Your heel hits one of the cans in the display, and they all come tumbling down. Cans roll everywhere.

What You Do

☐ You stand looking at the scene in shock, pretending to know nothing about it.
☐ You pick up the cans and pile them together.
☐ You walk to one of the checkers and report what has happened.
☐ You wait until a person who works at the store walks by, and then you apologize for what has happened.
☐ You hurry and leave the supermarket before anyone knows you did it.
☐ You do something else. What?

What Your Mom or Dad Would Want You to Do

Tell what this might be.

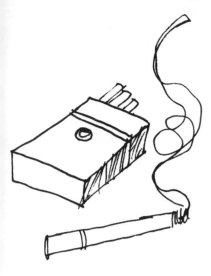

What You See

On Saturday morning you go to the park to play soccer with some friends. As you ride your bike to the edge of the field, you see that only three of your friends are there. Thirty minutes later, no others have come. One friend says that you need more players to have any fun. Another pulls out a pack of cigarettes and suggests that you all smoke and skip the game. The other two agree to try the cigarettes.

What You Do

☐ You decide to try one, tell them you don't like it, and quit.
☐ You don't want to lose friends, so you agree to go along.
☐ You tell your friends that smoking is a stupid thing to do and try to talk them out of it.
☐ You tell your friends that they can smoke but you'll just watch.
☐ You tell your friends good-bye and ride away on your bike.
☐ You do something else. What?

What Your Mom or Dad Would Want You to Do

Tell what this might be.

In reply to situations,
There are many words to tell.
The value in the effort
Is how to tell them well.

Skits

■ THESE SKITS are small dramas. If the group is not comfortable with actually acting out the drama, assign each speaking part to a youngster and have the drama read aloud.

At the end of each skit, five possible responses to the situation are given. Each response should be discussed. "What values are being communicated to others by the speaker?" "Is the speaker going along with acts or activities that are obviously right or obviously wrong?" The adult leader needs to facilitate discussion of each response.

After discussing all responses at the end of a skit, ask the youngsters to rank the responses from best to worst. Be alert to the possibility of further discussion developing as a result of this ranking exercise. The youngsters begin to realize that there are messages within the responses and that internal values can be inferred. Help them identify these messages and the values that may be hidden there. What messages convey the external values? Help the youngsters decide what the speaker is saying about how he or she wants to live.

The discussion should be open and risk-free to the extent that the youngsters are comfortable enough to speculate. Once the youngsters begin to display this kind of trust and freedom, gently challenge their responses with "Why?" "How?" "Do we all agree?" "Explain," or "Tell me more." Moderate pressure of this sort puts emphasis on the discovery of values.

Making an appropriate response in interpersonal exchanges takes practice. We all need opportunities for working through interpersonal exchanges to learn to make value-based responses.

SKITS

Chuck and Angelo sit with their backs against a large tree near the edge of an asphalt basketball court. Mario is sprawled on the ground near their feet.

ANGELO: Look who's coming!

MARIO: *(Raising himself on one elbow.)* You mean Richard?

ANGELO: Yeah, Richard.

CHUCK: Tell him to get lost! He's a lousy player. Let's wait for somebody else.

ANGELO: Oh, man, he can't catch. He can't dribble. He can't pass. He can't shoot. He can't even stay on his feet most of the time.

(All laugh)

CHUCK: Well, he's almost here. Let's just laugh at him until he leaves.

ANGELO: Good idea!

MARIO: *(Standing up)* No, that's not a good idea.

CHUCK: What d'ya mean? We gotta get rid of him, Mario.

ANGELO: Yeah, he's no fun to play with — he's just fun to laugh at.

Five different responses that Mario might make are listed below. Which responses might be good and appropriate? Why? Which responses might not be good? Why? Which response is best? Why?

1) "Richard has enough trouble. I'm not going to laugh at him."
2) "Yeah, I guess you guys are right. Let's get rid of him."
3) "Hey, guys, it's kinda lousy to make fun of anyone."
4) "If you guys wanna hurt Richard's feelings, go right ahead. I'm not going to."
5) "Just let Richard do the best he can. If you laugh at him, though, and he leaves, I'll go with him."

Holly, Erica, and Adele are relaxing in a booth at a fast-food restaurant. They each have a soft drink.

ERICA: Maybe we should have asked Jenny to come with us.

HOLLY: She'd just be chintzy again. I'm glad we slipped away without her.

ERICA: I suppose so. She wouldn't buy anything. She'd just sit there and watch us.

ADELE: Have you guys ever asked Jenny why she never spends any money on anything?

HOLLY: I haven't. I've tried to buy her something, but she always turns me down.

ERICA: Yeah, me, too. She makes me feel uncomfortable. Like, she sits there with no coke, no ice cream, no hamburger. I think I'll just dump her.

HOLLY: Good idea. It's more fun when she isn't along anyway.

ADELE: Hey, you two don't mean that!

ERICA: Of course we do, Adele. Why shouldn't we?

Five different responses that Adele might make are given below. Which responses might be good and appropriate? Why? Which responses might not be good? Why? Which response is best? Why?

1) "Well, maybe Jenny just never has any money to spend."
2) "Golly, I don't know. Dumping Jenny just seems like a bum thing to do."
3) "I think Jenny needs friends even more than we do."
4) "Okay, so do it your way. I'll go along."
5) "I don't think we should ever dump anyone. Jenny's a nice kid. She doesn't talk much, and she never spends money. Let her be herself and ask her to join us."

Five students are visiting with the principal in his office.

MR. FORD: So how are you eager youngsters doing?

NANCY: Well, we'd like to know when Miss Murphy is coming back. How is she doing?

MR. FORD: Miss Murphy is still very sick. She had a terrible accident, you know.

GAIL: Does that mean Mrs. Shaw is going to stay?

RON: Boy, I hope not!

MR. FORD: Don't you like Mrs. Shaw?

ALL: No way!

NANCY: Miss Murphy was so much fun, and she made learning fun. Mrs. Shaw never smiles.

FRED: She knows a lot, but she sits at her desk too much.

NANCY: Yeah. Miss Murphy was all over the room doing neat things.

BECKY: Mrs. Shaw moves around only a little bit. Is there something wrong with her leg? She only stands for a little while and then she sits down behind her desk and rubs her leg.

MR. FORD: Yes, Becky, as a matter of fact, Mrs. Shaw used to be a very active teacher. Three years ago she was run down by a hit-and-run driver. She suffered a severe fracture of her leg. I asked her to try teaching again when Miss Murphy had her accident. Her leg never healed right and it gives her a lot of pain.

Five different responses that Becky might make are listed below. Which responses might be good and appropriate? Why? Which responses might not be good? Why? Which response is best?

1) "Okay. Then we have to work with Mrs. Shaw so she can teach us better. She does know a lot."

2) "Well then, Mrs. Shaw should quit. It will be hard for us to learn much from her if she's hurting all the time."

3) "I understand, but school is no fun with her."

4) "Why didn't she tell us that she had a sore leg?"

5) "What a bummer! We lose Miss Murphy and get stuck with Mrs. Shaw for the rest of the school year."

Mavis, Lola, and Kim are lounging in Kim's bedroom after school.

LOLA: Cathy is a rat. I just can't believe it.

KIM: Oh, she's the one that squealed, all right. Then she avoided me the rest of the day.

MAVIS: How can we be so sure?

KIM: I saw her watching us, and when she took her paper to Miss Collins, the teacher looked right at me while Cathy was talking to her.

MAVIS: Okay. What else?

LOLA: Right after that, Miss Collins compared our papers and asked us to stay to see her at recess.

KIM: Yeah, and then the way Cathy avoided us all day.

LOLA: Hey, if that's the way she wants to be, I say give it to her. Give her the silent treatment. I think we should just not ever talk to her again.

MAVIS: *(Laughing)* That sounds like an awful long time!

KIM: Well, I agree with Lola. We should freeze her out and get other kids to do the same.

Five different responses that Mavis might make are listed below. Which responses might be good and appropriate? Why? Which responses might not be good? Why? Which response is best? Why?

1) "Hey, I don't think we want to do that. After all, we did cheat."
2) "Well, I disagree. I don't think we're even sure Cathy ratted on us. Maybe Miss Collins is smarter than we think."
3) "Yeah, it looks like Cathy did tell on us. That sure wasn't being a good friend."
4) "I'm going to ask her if she ratted on us. Then I'll decide what to do."
5) "Not me! I cheated and I feel awful. I won't make it worse by picking on Cathy."

Walt, Norman, and Kent are sitting on a large rock in the outcropping that forms part of Lincoln Park.

KENT: How did you find out about this?

NORMAN: My big brother told me. His girlfriend moved to Omaha, and when he went to visit her, he found it out. Mr. Coleman was a teacher there.

WALT: I just can't believe the coach is a convict.

NORMAN: He got sent to jail for a year.

WALT: What did he do?

NORMAN: He was a teacher and a coach at a high school. One day he caught a dope peddler hanging around when the kids were practicing. He beat him up so bad, he almost killed him. My brother said he was sentenced to a year in jail but got out in six months.

KENT: Wouldn't they let him teach anymore? Why did he come here to work in a garage?

NORMAN: I don't know. I just hope someone doesn't make him quit being our coach.

WALT: Is your brother going to tell all the parents? Some of them might get pretty mad!

NORMAN: Not yet. He told me he would watch our practices, and I should tell him if Mr. Coleman does anything funny. If Coach acts okay, he's not going to say anything.

KENT: Do you think we have to tell anybody?

Five different responses that Walt might make are listed below. Which responses might be good and appropriate? Why? Which responses might not be good? Why? Which response is best? Why?

1) "We should zip our lip tight so we don't lose our soccer coach."
2) "I think we have to tell our parents. If my dad found out I knew this and didn't tell him, he'd be angry."
3) "Norman's brother knows. That's enough."
4) "Coach is trying to get a new start. If we tell, it'd be like a TV show I saw. We'd ruin him."
5) "If we tell, we might lose our coach. If we don't tell, he might beat up one of us. We have to tell our parents."

Four girls are walking along the sidewalk, giggling and talking.

VAL: Yeah, it was a funny movie. I'm glad our teacher isn't as goofy as theirs was, though.

APRIL: Look! Hamburger Haven's coming up. I'll buy you guys a coke or an ice cream.

POLLY: I don't know. I promised to come straight home.

LOUISE: Me, too.

APRIL: Sure, I promised, too. But stopping for a treat is still going straight home.

VAL: That's right. Our folks just don't want us goofing off along the street at night.

LOUISE: Well, I guess so. If I tell my mom when I get home, it would probably be all right.

POLLY: I can't do it. My dad explained that coming straight home means no stops. I have to go on home.

VAL: But you can't go home alone. We promised to stay together. Come on, Polly. We won't stay long.

APRIL: Come on, Polly. It'll be fun.

Five different responses that Polly might make are listed below. Which responses might be good or appropriate? Why? Which responses might not be good? Why? Which response is best? Why?

1) "You guys are making me disobey. I can't stop to eat ice cream."
2) "No way! If you all stop, I'll have to go on home alone."
3) "I suppose you're right. It is safer to stay together, even if we are a little late."
4) "Louise, you said you had to go right home. Why don't you come with me?"
5) "Oh, nobody will ever know. Let's eat ice cream!"

Bruce, Phil, and Zach enjoy sweet rolls as they sit in the booth at the pancake shop.

PHIL: These are good. I've never had 'em before.

BRUCE: Oh, I come here whenever I get hungry.

ZACH: What? Get real! These things cost a buck each!

BRUCE: So.

ZACH: So, where d'ya get all the money?

BRUCE: The easy way, man. Out of my mom's purse.

ZACH: You mean you steal it?

BRUCE: It ain't exactly stealing. I just take a couple bucks when I need 'em. Hey, look. I only use it for food — and she's supposed to feed me, isn't she? Besides, she never misses it.

ZACH: You're crazy! How many times have you done that?

BRUCE: Gee, I don't even know anymore.

ZACH: Wonder if my mom would miss money if I took some from her purse. Maybe I'll try it.

Five different responses that Phil might make are listed below. Which responses might be good or appropriate? Why? Which responses might not be good? Why? Which response is best? Why?

1) "Me, too! It sounds like a great way to get some extra allowance."
2) "What's up with you guys? It doesn't matter what you spend it for — it's still stealing."
3) "Listen, Bruce, if that's how you paid for this treat, I'm sorry I came."
4) "I think you're both joking. You know better than to steal from your own mom."
5) "Not me, Zach, and you better not either. If Bruce wants to be a thief, let him. But that's no reason for us to be one, too."

It's Sunday afternoon. Natalie, Sheila, and Libby are sitting in Libby's yard after a long bike ride.

NATALIE: Libby, we missed you at my slumber party last night.

LIBBY: Yeah, I'm sorry. My aunt and uncle were here and the whole family went out to dinner and then to a movie.

NATALIE: There was just Sheila and Margo and me. Without you to liven things up, it was pretty quiet!

SHEILA: That's right. We needed you with your wisecracks and your ideas for silly games. I couldn't sleep, I kept thinking about Margo.

LIBBY: What about Margo?

SHEILA: Her stepdad beats her. She showed us some bad marks when she put on her p.j.'s. Her back and her ribs were all black and blue.

LIBBY: Didn't she tell some adult about that?

NATALIE: No. He told her that if she ever ratted on him, he'd give her a lot worse.

SHEILA: She made us promise not to tell. You can't tell either.

LIBBY: Okay. But we have to find some way to help her. He's abusing her.

SHEILA: Sure, we know that. But if we turn him in to someone, he might kill her.

Five different responses that Libby might make are listed below. Which responses might be good or appropriate? Why? Which responses might not be good? Why? Which response is best? Why?

1) "That's why we should do something. My neighbor is a detective. Maybe we should talk to him."
2) "You're right. If we go to somebody, we might just make it worse for Margo."
3) "I guess if she hasn't told anybody, then we shouldn't tell anyone either."
4) "Listen. We have to help Margo. I don't know how, but I think we ought to talk to my mom right now."
5) "I have an idea. Tomorrow I'll do something to get Mrs. Dawson to send me to the principal. Then I'll tell him about Margo. He's smart enough to help her without getting Margo hurt."

Paula, Gloria, and Celeste are taking a shortcut through the park on their way home from school. When they pass near a bench, they sit down to rest.

GLORIA: I can't think very well and walk at the same time. Let's rest a minute.

CELESTE: Good idea. Miss Nelson says we can't do anything about it. The superintendent said no more field trips.

GLORIA: Yeah, and that robs us of our Nature Day.

PAULA: That's the only field trip for us all year long. It just isn't fair.

CELESTE: We're getting cheated! Our grade has had Nature Day since they built the school. Now the superintendent takes it away from us. Why don't they save money some other way?

GLORIA: My mom says he has to save money because people voted no on the election.

CELESTE: But why does he have to pick on us?

GLORIA: When my dad called him, he said he doesn't have enough money, so he has to cancel using buses for field days.

PAULA: Isn't there something we can do?

CELESTE: Oh, sure! You always have lots of ideas. You tell us what we can do.

Five different responses that Paula might make are listed below. Which responses might be good or appropriate? Why? Which responses might not be good? Why? Which response is best? Why?

1) "Well, when they wanted to bus some of us across town to go to school, the parents got people to sign a paper. We could do that."
2) "All the kids in our grade could go to the superintendent's office and tell him to give us back our Nature Day."
3) "Remember Mr. Baxter? He gave our class those computers. He has lots of flowers and shrubs and grass at the factory he owns. We don't need buses to go there. We can walk and have Nature Day with his gardener."
4) "Miss Nelson is probably right. We should just give up."
5) "Let's write a letter to the editor of the newspaper. We can tell the whole town how we've been let down."

Fred, Clay, Ethan, and Gordon sit at the table in the cafeteria at school. Fred's arm is in a sling.

GORDON: Boy, this is a good lunch today!

CLAY: *(Laughing)* Not for Fred. He needs two hands to eat his spaghetti.

FRED: It's okay, funny guy! I can eat one-handed, left-handed.

ETHAN: Sorry you have to. If that old lady had cleared away her snow, you wouldn't have slipped.

GORDON: That's right. She's the only one along that stretch who doesn't clean her walks. Five blocks and only one house.

CLAY: Yeah. People walk on the snow, it turns to ice, and then Fred falls on it.

FRED: I was pretty clumsy. You guys didn't fall.

GORDON: Sure, man, but you wouldn't have fallen either if that old lady had cleared her walk.

ETHAN: Let's just hope nobody else gets hurt.

CLAY: Yeah. How can it be helped, though?

Five different responses that Ethan might make are listed below. Which responses might be good or appropriate? Why? Which responses might not be good? Why? Which response is best? Why?

1) "Just do what we do sometimes: walk in the street."
2) "We could probably call somebody and complain, but the old lady probably can't do it herself and hasn't enough money to get somebody else to do it."
3) "We could ring her doorbell and ask her to please clean her walks."
4) "Why don't we each write her a letter and tell her about what happened to Fred?"
5) "Whenever it snows, why don't we all get our shovels and clean her walk for her?"

Let us sing a song together
About values old and new.
Let us share a happy moment
As we think our values through.

Parodies

■ A PARODY is an exaggeration or a spoof on something otherwise serious — like different words sung to a familiar tune.

Singing together is an old method of helping individuals develop the spirit and skill of thinking together. It's also just plain fun.

With the understanding of what a parody is and an appreciation for the unique affect group singing can create, you're ready to help kids discover values in parodies.

We want kids to be aware of two kinds of values: internal and external (inside values and outside values). The internal, or inside values, are what we perceive as good and worth going after. External, or outside values, involve behavior that tells others how we want to live.

Review the material in the Introduction. We looked at ways to define these values. Throughout each section of this workbook, we remind, review, repeat, emphasize, and reinforce these definitions to provide youngsters with a clear and objective picture of values and how to discover them. These final exercises add a unique flavor of fun.

Sing the following words to the tune noted in each song. Ideally, you and the kids should commit the songs to memory. A piano or guitar accompanist will add to the fun and enhance the learning potential of everyone involved.

After you and the kids have laughed and giggled your way through a song, begin looking for the messages that convey values. Engage the kids in a series of questions that will generate value-based responses. Questions provided at the end of each parody are designed to stimulate discussion.

As with previous exercises, we want to encourage the kids to think about what values are and how influential they are in determining behavior. In this section, we mix in the fun of singing together with a last look at discovering values.

Singing is an ancient form of expression. When people gather to sing together, a warm interaction is generated in young and old alike. Such an atmosphere provides an opening for informal but serious value-based discussions.

Kindness

(to the tune "My Bonnie Lies Over the Ocean")

Being kind is topnotch behavior.
Being kind is the best way to be.
Being kind is a way to be proud of.
O kindness come right back to me!

Come back, come back,
Come back my kindness to me, to me.
Come back, come back,
O come back my kindness to me!

Is kindness something a person can act out, something good a person can do? Explain.

Do you think of kindness as a value? Why?

If we show kindness to people, are they usually kind to us? What does the song tell us about this?

Being unselfish works a lot like being kind. Think of another value that is like these two. Tell how they are all alike.

Sing the song again at the end of the discussion.

Working

(to the tune "My Bonnie Lies Over the Ocean")

Keep working if you would be happy.
Keep working if you want success.
Keep working if you would be happy.
Don't surrender to old laziness!

Bring back, bring back,
Bring back achievement to me, to me.
Bring back, bring back,
O bring back achievement to me!

Is working something good that a person can do? Explain.

How do you think achievement is related to working?

Do you think working and achievement are values? Why?

The song tells you to avoid "old laziness." Is laziness a good value? Could
it be a bad value? Explain.

How do you sometimes act out laziness?

Sing the song again at the end of the discussion.

Caring

(to the tune of the refrain "Battle Hymn of the Republic")

Caring! Caring! For my neighbor!
Caring! Caring! For my neighbor!
Caring! Caring! For my neighbor!
Will help us both march on.

(Sing additional verses substituting "neighbor" with "mother," "father," "buddy," "brother," "sister," and "teacher.")

Is caring something a person can act out, something good a person can do? Explain.

Do you think of caring as a value? Why?

The persons in the song are all persons you are close to and know well. Can you and should you care for people you don't know well? Explain.

How do you show others that you care for them?

Sing the song again at the end of the discussion.

Honesty

(to the tune "Jingle Bells")

Telling truth tonight
In an honest sort of way
Makes everything all right
Tomorrow and today.
Let me never lie
Whatever I might gain.
I'll never have to justify
Rewards that I attain...Oh...

Tell the truth! Tell the truth!
Truthful all my days!
Oh, how great to know I speak
With an honest voice always.
Tell the truth! Tell the truth!
Truthful all my days!
Oh, how great to know I speak
With an honest voice always.

The song says it's "great to know I speak with an honest voice." Why, do you think, is it great to know that?

Is telling the truth important to you? Why or why not?

How do you feel when someone doesn't tell you the truth?

Why can you call honesty a value?

Sing the song again at the end of the discussion.

Helping

(to the tune "Jingle Bells")

Helping others cope
With the problems that they face,
Giving others hope,
Troubles to erase.
Having friends you've known,
Helping with your fight.
How hard it is to be alone
When things just don't go right...Oh...

Giving help! Giving help!
Helping all the way!
Oh, what satisfaction comes
When you help some friend each day.
Giving help! Giving help!
Brings a happy smile.
Oh, what fun to know you help
In an open, giving style.

Do you agree or disagree with what the song says? Why?

Should we just help others or should we expect them to help us in return?
Explain.

Should we always help or are there times when it might be better not to
help? Explain.

Helping is not always easy to do. Do you think we should do more helping
when it's easy and less when it's hard? Why?

Sing the song again at the end of the discussion.

Obedience

(to the tune "Three Blind Mice")

Three good boys,
Three good boys.
See them obey,
See them obey.
They act as their father tells them to,
They work till the chores are finished and through.
Do you see all the good jobs these three boys can do?
The three good boys.

Is obedience a value that helps you choose how to behave? Tell how this works.

How does the song tell us that obedience makes the boys good?

Do you always find it easy to obey? Explain.

Some folks are especially pleased when others obey. Why, do you think, does this happen?

How does it make you feel when you obey?

Sing the song again at the end of the discussion.

Vandalism

(to the tune "Three Blind Mice")

Don't throw rocks,
Don't throw rocks.
See who it hurts,
See who it hurts.
It hurts the one whose property's lost.
It bothers us all 'cause it raises the cost.
It's vandalism whene'er a rock is tossed
Through a window pane.

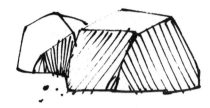

What does "respect for the property of others" mean?

Define the word *vandalism.*

When you are being thoughtless, is vandalism fun? Why or why not?

When you are being thoughtful, is vandalism fun? Why or why not?

Can you think of vandalism as a bad value? Why?

Sing the song again at the end of the discussion.

Cheating

(to the tune "Auld Lang Syne")

Should any cheating be forgot
On tests of any kind?
Should study take the place of fraud
In opening my mind?
O what I learn is mine, my friend,
O what I learn is mine.
We'll do a bit of study now
For what I learn is mine!

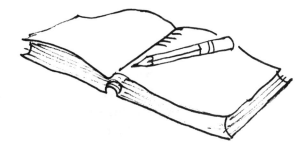

The song asks a question: "Should study take the place of fraud in opening my mind?" What does this say to you?

If you cheat to get something, is it really yours? Explain.

When you study and learn something new, is it really yours? Why?

Do you think a cheater would make a good friend? Why?

When someone cheats, does that tell others something about the way that person wants to live? Explain.

Sing the song again at the end of the discussion.

Prayers

(to the tune "Auld Lang Syne")

If all my cares become too great
For me to handle well,
Then prayers I'll say to ask for aid
And haunting doubts dispel.
For prayers to God can help, my friend,
For prayers to God will help.
We'll live a happy, prayer-filled life,
'Cause prayers to God do help.

In what ways can praying be considered a value?

If you are a prayerful person, what are you telling others about how you want to live your life?

If you are willing to rely on prayer, what other values do you probably have? Explain.

Does the song tell you that praying will help solve problems? How?

Is praying important in your life? Tell about it.

Sing the song again at the end of the discussion.

Shoplifting

(to the tune "Take Me Out to the Ball Game")

Teach me never to shoplift.
Teach me to pay my own way.
Help me to just simply realize
I can't just run off with a prize.
For it's pay, pay, pay through the check line.
If you don't pay, there's a fine.
For its one, two, three, then to jail
For the shoplift crime.

Why do some people shoplift?

Explain why shoplifting is considered a bad value.

Why is it sometimes hard to avoid bad values?

Do people usually shoplift things that are not attractive? What does this tell us?

Would a shoplifter be a good person to have as a friend? Why or why not?

Sing the song again at the end of the discussion.

More Helpful Resources From Liguori...

The Hidden Fortune
by Bill Dodds

In this novel, young readers will meet seventh–grader, Jeannette. When "weird old uncle Jackie" moves in, Jeannette is forced to make some sacrifices, including her room! But a mystery soon develops over whether her great–uncle, who looks like a penniless bum, is actually an eccentric millionaire. She even wonders if she should be nice to him in the hopes of inheriting his fortune. Jeannette ultimately learns that people are more important than possessions and that the best fortune is not a material one. **$4.95**

In My Heart Room, Book One — *16 Love Prayers for Little Children*
by Mary Terese Donze, ASC

Written for parents and teachers of 6- to 10-year-olds, this book offers a simple, easy-to-follow method of teaching children a special way to pray. First, the children are instructed to concentrate on an everyday item like a pencil, a penny, or a flower. They are then gently led from concentration to meditation and into their "heart's room" to be close to God. **$1.95**

In My Heart Room, Book Two — *More Love Prayers for Children*
by Mary Terese Donze, ASC

Like the original book, this book presents more "guided imagery" prayers. Parents and teachers can lead children through 16 more prayer experiences focusing on simple objects like a balloon, a garden, and others. Also adaptable for older children and adults. **$2.95**

Advent Is for Children — *Stories, Activities, Prayers*
by Julie Kelemen

Here is an ideal way to help middle-graders prepare for the celebration of Christmas. This book contains attention-grabbing stories, fun activities, and thoughtful prayers to help young people understand how and why we celebrate Advent. Children learn to see past all the glitter and wrapping to the true gift of Christ. **$1.95**

Lent Is for Children — *Stories, Activities, Prayers*
by Julie Kelemen

Like its Advent counterpart, this book helps middle-graders discover not just the "how tos" but the "whys" of the season. It offers practices, activities, and prayers that explain and reinforce Lenten basics like fasting, self-sacrifice, reconciliation, and more. **$1.95**

VIDEO

Let the Children Come to Me — *The Word of God Alive for Children*
produced by Redemptorist Pastoral Communications

Father Joe Kempf (featured in *A Child's First Penance* and *A Child's First Communion*) presents 12 brief Scripture-based homilies for children. Teachers and children alike will find inspiration in this video. It is an excellent example of how simple props, thoughtful preparation, and the active involvement of children can greatly increase young people's understanding of Scripture and help make God's Word come alive in their minds and hearts. Vignettes can be viewed individually. Comes with a teacher's guide complete with discussion questions. **$49.95**

Order from your local bookstore or write to
Liguori Publications
Box 060, Liguori, MO 63057-9999
For faster service call (800) 325-9521, ext. 060, 8 a.m. to 4 p.m. Central time.
(Please add $1 for postage and handling to orders under $5,
$1.50 to orders between $5 and $15; $2 to orders over $15.)